HIDDEN MEANINGS

Gerald Walker Smith

CELESTIAL ARTS
MILLBRAE, CALIFORNIA

First Printing, May 1977
Made in the United States of America

Library of Congress Cataloging in Publication Data

Smith, Gerald Walker.
  Hidden meanings.

  1. Interpersonal relations.   2. Communication—Social
aspects.   I. Title.
[HM132.S55 1977]   301.14   76-56897
ISBN 0-89087-149-3

1 2 3 4 5 6 7 — 81 80 79 78 77

Contents

III Hidden Meanings Between Parent and Child 37

IV Hidden Meanings Between Friends 57

viii

V Hidden Meanings Between Associates and Acquaintances 95

ix

xi

Acknowledgments

My thanks to John Levy for his judgment on a number of drafts of this book. Thanks also to Noel Morrell, Michael Murphy, David Schwartz, Hank Basayne and Jim McAllister—all offered helpful suggestions during the writing. Our "extended family" of Dan and Maureen Cooper, David and Karen Crommie, Helen Gibbs, Walter and Esther Johnson, Ed Leon, B.B. and Barbara Lyon, and Dick Raines were particularly helpful during the final draft. Barbara Wyden's creative and editorial contribution was important during the initial stages of writing.

Throughout the work, my wife, Linda's eye for writing and ear for what people said was a great help.

Gerald Smith
San Mateo, California

To
Linda
AND
Bib,
Andy,
Margo
AND
Martin.

I

*The Meaning
Behind the Meaning
Behind the Meaning*

"*I* hear what you're saying, but what are you saying?"

This is not the contradiction it seems to be. Words can become such a dense screen to obscure our real meanings, thoughts and feelings that more and more psychologists, semanticists, and psycholinguists are at work trying to find out what people really *are* saying.

What's behind their words?

What's the true meaning?

Researchers are also examining what people unwittingly reveal about themselves, their characters, their fears, their hostilities, their concerns when they communicate with certain words and phrases.

Nowadays, as "communications" turns into a science of sorts, many people, paradoxically, seem less and less able to exchange authentic feelings, emotions, information about their physical and psychological states. We take refuge behind clichés, quips, silences, lies, obscurities. Some are even too shy or

1

inhibited or otherwise unable to tell others what they
want or need. Naturally, whoever listens to such
people is unable to decode their messages. Both par-
ties to such noncommunication are being left out in
the cold.

Even people who love each other run into such
dead ends or worse. It is not unusual for husbands
and wives or lovers, for instance, to express their tenderness through rather cruel raillery. A husband may
say to his wife, "You're absolutely impossible. You're a
bitch." His wife might take him seriously. If he is
lucky, she will understand by the way he holds his
body, the tone of his voice, the look in his eyes, that he
means exactly the opposite of what he's saying.

But why can't he say what he truly means?

Why can't he say, "I think you're a wonderful
woman. I love your openness, your cheerfulness. And
I think you are tremendously sexy."

Because he can't. It would make him uncomfortable.

But why should it? Why is he frightened of revealing his love?

The answers are clear to those who know how to
look behind words, who know how to peel off the
deceptive outer layer of communication. Suppose the
husband is not sure that his love is reciprocated. He
worries that his wife is not as wholeheartedly admir-
ing of him as he is of her. Therefore, he covers his
declaration of love with a self-protective, defensive
statement: "You're . . . impossible . . . a bitch." And
he actually expects his wife to decode this into a love
message. It happens every day.

But suppose that even though she loves him
dearly his phrasing is so negative that it prevents her
from expressing her love. Then he may never dis-

cover that she really does love him every bit as much as he loves her. By trying to insulate himself from hurt, he has insulated himself from joy. And while one can survive most wounds, one can never counterfeit joy. The husband becomes a loser because he does not dare to say what he means and feels.

But wait! There are still more meanings here than meet the ear. The "bitch" message, like many (possibly the majority of) messages between two people, carries meanings wrapped within meanings or, to paraphrase Winston Churchill, "riddles within enigmas."

The wife must translate "bitch" as "wonderful woman," but why did he choose the term "bitch"? Why didn't he call her a "silly goose," for instance—a somewhat more endearing image?

The fact is that he is putting her down. He is saying that if she does not reciprocate his love, she is a bitch, less than human—and unworthy of him.

He is also conveying a suggestion that he may feel unworthy of being loved—that he thinks the only person who could possibly love him absolutely has to be a bitch because he himself is so unworthy.

This may sound like an untypically complicated example, but it is in fact no more complicated than many of the coded messages that are exchanged between strangers, colleagues, acquaintances and intimates every day. It is a demonstration of the way people build an invisible wall around themselves. But—and this is the principal point of this book—the "bitch" message suggests the rewards of being direct and saying what you mean.

This husband cheated himself out of the joy of being certain he is loved—for fear that he might learn that he is not. True, this husband must be strong in order to accept the truth behind the words. But it is ever so much easier to face the light of truth than it is to face the dark of the unknown. One can build on truth; one can move on from it. The unknown is quicksand; you never know where you stand. Fearful fantasies weave themselves around the unknown— and this is much more destructive than any truth could ever be.

Words rarely mean exactly what we say. The result is a retreat behind wording that disguises meaning and insulates men, women and children from real understanding of each other. We have reached the point where it has become a matter of first rank importance to decipher our everyday exchanges and find out what most of us really mean by such commonplace expressions as:

Just a minute.
What are you doing tonight?
Did you come?
You make me mad.
In my judgment . . .

I want to help you find a way to breach the invisible walls that grow higher and thicker each time we fearfully resort to verbal symbols to obscure our meanings and feelings. It will not be easy: first, to understand what others are really saying; second, to learn how to communicate clearly, unambiguously and fearlessly. But the payoffs of better mutual understanding are beyond compare.

How does one go about all this? How can one learn to decode people's words, to find out what they really mean? The entries in this book of hidden meanings will supply the keys needed to decipher most of the everyday expressions that people hide behind. Although the English language is capable of an infinite number of sentences, those sentences and phrases that are what psycholinguists call "psychologically plausible" are relatively few. Most phrases fall into more or less readily identifiable categories. And once the reader learns to recognize the categories and understands how to decode conversational interchanges, most messages become transparent and meaningful. Decoding becomes almost second nature.

This is not surprising. The way the human mind works, while magnificent and awe-inspiring, need not confound us. It is our own mind, after all. By knowing ourselves and being in touch with our own feelings, we are already halfway toward understanding other people and their feelings—and toward knowing what they are really saying.

Words are symbols. Behind the symbols lurk many meanings. Some are obvious. Some are hostile and threatening. Others are evasive and frightened. Some are joyous and exulting. Some are calls for help. This compendium defines words, phrases and sentences of everyday usage that usually carry several levels of meaning.

I have tried to break down the psychological content of these messages to help you decode what someone really means when he or she sends you such messages as, "Give me a kiss," or, "Be a man!" or asks "What does he see in her?"

The reader who looks up the phrases from his conversational repertoire and from conversations of the people he encounters daily should be able to:

1. Find out what the other person really means most of the time.

2. Guard against being diminished into a put-down position.
3. Guard against being manipulated.
4. Communicate more directly and honestly with others to get on the same wavelength and avoid misunderstandings.
5. Help others communicate more directly and honestly for the same purposes.

One key to becoming aware of hidden meanings is a simple question that is worth asking frequently:

Does what I hear the person say fit with the way he says it—his voice, his posture, his rate of speech, his gestures, the look in his eyes, the turn of his mouth?

In short, is there matching between what he says and how he says it.

Think back and remember times when people you talked with were saying things that did not match their behavior.

How about the person who said, "I'm sorry," but didn't look to you as if he were sorry at all? It seemed that he was just mouthing the words. His face didn't show sorrow, nor did his voice. When that happened there surely was a hidden meaning underneath the actual words.

Following each entry in this book are a number of possibilities for what is really being said—the hidden meaning.

Which of these meanings applies in any particular situation in your life? I cannot tell you that with certainty, just as no dictionary can tell you which of several definitions for even the simplest word may apply in a particular context. A choice between possible meanings must be made. Only you can make that choice. But this book will show you how.

Before you decide on any interpretation of a hidden meaning, always consider not only the other person's words, but his or her voice, face, gestures, actions, etc. These factors, too, can obviously be helpful tip-offs to you when you are working to establish the true meaning of what is being said.

In some instances you will probably want to work out your own meaning, one that is not in this dictionary, but the principles in this book will be helpful in deciding on a meaning that makes the most sense to you.

What this book will not do is to try to teach you how to read another person's mind. It is simply a guide to understanding what he is saying. To try to read another person's mind, to "psychologize" him, is an egregious trespass into that person's most private property, his mind.

No one has the right to try to read another's mind. It is far more important for all of us that we first find out what is in our own heads—to work at becoming more sensitive to our own feelings. I believe that if a person knows himself, he can quickly and legitimately find out all that he needs to know about others.

Naturally the principles in this book apply to both males and females. The use of combination pronouns such as "he/she" and "him/her" are at times awkward and reduce clarity. Therefore I have frequently used either male or female pronouns.

Note to the reader: Hidden Meanings, because of its nature, is an ongoing process and, hence, necessarily incomplete. I have tried to avoid those words and phrases that seem headed for immediate obsolescence, but have included those "slang" usages that

seem to have become a part of the language. But I'm
sure I have omitted some phrases that are obvious
candidates for such a book. I invite you therefore, to
participate with me in the preparation of the next
edition of *Hidden Meanings*. Suggestions for new entries, as well as criticisms and corrections of existing
entries, will be welcomed and carefully considered.
Letters may be addressed as follows:

Hidden Meanings
c/o Celestial Arts
231 Adrian Road
Millbrae, California 94030.

II

Hidden Meanings Between Lovers

*T*he stakes are highest when hidden meanings occur in communication between lovers—much more so than between friends or acquaintances. Obviously, lovers possess great power for hurting each other because they are most vulnerable to each other.

Take, for example, the first meaning in the section to follow: "Did you come?" The emotional content is so high in this message (at least in some relationships) that many a woman will lie and say she did come to an orgasm. Often the lying erodes the entire relationship because the woman loses spontaneity sexually and instead feels she must perform for the man's benefit. In short, sexual lying undermines the woman's self-esteem as a whole person, not only as a sexual person. In addition, sexual lying breeds deep resentment against the man.

Between acquaintances, it often does not make much difference if some meanings remain hidden. But between lovers the fewer the hidden meanings, the better the chance for an open, enduring and mutually satisfying relationship.

"Did you come?"

This is a man's question. And, usually, a loaded one. Here is what it may mean:

☐ The stud is saying, "Well, go on, tell me! Your orgasm isn't yours. It's mine. I gave it to you. I worked for it. And I want you to acknowledge it."

☐ The uptight lover is really saying, "Sex is to have an orgasm. Sex is serious. The goal is more important than the journey." If his sex partner did not have an orgasm, Mr. Uptight tends to feel he is inadequate.

☐ The timid (or inexperienced) lover is saying, "Please say yes! You have to come. If you don't, it means I'm inadequate. And I can't stand that. Next time I may not even be able to get it up. Say yes. Please."

☐ The loving lover is saying, "I hope you liked it as much as I did. But I have to tell you that I got so excited that I was carried away. I lost track of you. Did you come? If you didn't, I'm sorry. But next time will be different. I love you, you know. And you made me feel terrific!"

"Do you mind if I have another drink?"

☐ This can be a legitimate question. But if the person feels it is necessary to ask it, a better way would be, "How do you feel about my having another drink?" When the question is put this way the questioner is not asking permission, but asking how the other person feels about that next drink. But why is he asking? Is it a matter of time? Would he like to have a drink before starting some other activity? Or is he trying to find out how the other person feels about his drinking before he drives someplace? Or is he letting the host know he would like another drink—in fact, he wants one badly enough to all but demand it.

If the speaker has a drinking problem and is married to a nurturing person who will give him permission to have that additional drink, this is a clue to an unhealthy symbiotic relationship that often exists in a marriage between an alcoholic and a nonalcoholic. The nondrinker is as dependent on the other being a drinker as the alcoholic is upon the "martyred" partner who puts up with him. In many cases, if the drinker cuts down on his heavy drinking, the marriage breaks up, because the other partner has lost his or her supportive role—to which the nondrinker is as addicted as the drinker is to alcohol.

☐ This question may carry an enormous load of guilt and be defensive, too. The speaker feels guilty about the way he behaves when he drinks too much, the way he acts and talks to people he loves. And yet he keeps on drinking. Some people literally drink themselves to death because it's the only way they can deal with their guilt.

How does one handle this question? By telling the truth. It is important to state:

    "I do *mind if you have another drink. I'm all ready to serve dinner."*
    or,
    "I do *mind. I am worried about you having to drive home."*
    or,
    "I do *mind. I am very worried about how much you're drinking and what it's doing to you." These responses may have no immediate effect on the drinker, but they will at least let him know that you are concerned about him, that you worry about his well-being. This is an important message to convey.*

"Do you mind if I have a sexual relationship with John/Joan?"

☐ Incredible as this might sound, people who have carried the quest for "honesty" to the absurd really do ask this question. If the other person cares deeply about the speaker and would be very distressed if the speaker had a sexual relationship with someone else, he/she can only reply by honestly voicing this distress.

☐ Sometimes the speaker is not willing to take full responsibility for a sexual relationship and therefore asks permission of the spouse/lover. The speaker wants to have it both ways. To embark on the new sexual relationship and also to continue the primary relationship without having to feel guilty. To top it off, such seekers of honesty may store up the other person's refusal to grant permission so that in years to come they can "play it back" to themselves and feed their resentment.

☐ This is a test question, and it does not actually concern an extramarital relationship but instead is an attempt to find out where the speaker stands with the partner. It would be less dangerous if the person said directly, "I don't know where I stand with you right now."

☐ In the case of an "open marriage," there might be a place for such a trial balloon. If so, it would be better phrased, "How would you feel if I had a sexual relationship with so and so?" This is preferable to asking permission.

Affairs often serve a purpose in marriage, a final effort to get the spouse's attention. Therefore, he/she has to have the partner find out, hence, a nude photo in the top drawer of the dresser under some papers, or a revealing letter to the wife from the other woman.

"Give me a kiss."

☐ Between lovers it's often a signal that the speaker is in need of reassurance. He or she feels insecure, even unloved, and wants a tangible expression of affection.

Why is one person demanding a kiss from the other person? If he/she wants a kiss why isn't that person initiating it rather than sitting back and asking that a kiss be delivered? If you are getting this "Give me a kiss" message from your partner, beware of the control that comes with the message. A kiss is a gift. Do you want to be in a position of delivering a gift on demand? Tell your partner how you feel when you get this message. The best way to do this is with "I" messages.

☐ "Give me a kiss" is sometimes simply playful talk between lovers.

"I" MESSAGES

The "I" message is essential for talk between lovers because it allows the most openness in expressing feelings. It is clear, and usually straightforward and easy to understand in contrast to "You" messages.

An "I" message rarely puts the listener on the defensive. This means that he is able to listen to what is being said without having to devote part of his thoughts to preparing to defend himself.

For instance: "You ought to go on a diet."

This is an attack. The listener understands that the speaker thinks he is too fat. There is also a further meaning hidden here: maybe the speaker is hinting that he does not think the other person will go on a diet, and that if he does go on a diet, the speaker does not think that the other person will stick to it.

An "I" message would go something like: "I'm worried about your weight. You say you've gained a lot recently."

No one welcomes being told (no matter how tactfully) that he is too fat, but this is not an attack or a criticism. It is a sincere statement that shows concern. It opens the door to further communication.

The overweight person can say, "I know. I suppose I should see the doctor, but I know he'll tell me to go on a diet and I don't think I can stay on one. Not right now anyway."

Another reply to this would be: "You're probably right, but I don't feel like it right now. Let's drop the subject."

Either way, the relationship between speaker and listener remains open and intimate. The concern is appreciated.

"I" messages tend to increase intimacy and clarify communication. "You" messages usually do the opposite.

Think in terms of a line or fence between you and the other person. With "I" messages you are staying on your side of the fence, because your feelings are within your territory. With "you" messages you trespass into the other person's territory, and hence invite defensiveness.

But, not all "I" messages are straightforward. Among the following entries there are several examples of twisted "I" messages. And this honest little pronoun can be the most deceitful of all. See Chapter VI: How to Guard Against the Deceptive Pronouns.

"I don't have a thing to wear."

☐ "I don't know what the others will be wearing and I feel that I'll be out of place."

☐ "I don't feel able to cope with a social situation if I don't have something new to wear." This person feels that people judge others by their clothes, because she/he makes that kind of judgment.

☐ It can also be a ploy to get the other person to buy something or say, "Go ahead, get something new." Hinting around like this, if it is a general pattern in the relationship, limits the relationship. It would be healthier if the two people talked as equals with a straightforward message such as:
"I want to get something new for the party."
or,

"I want to buy something new for the party. How do you feel about that idea?"

"I don't know you well enough yet."

☐ We all know what this means. She's not going to bed with the fellow. Not on this date anyway. But this classic female excuse for refusing sex has nothing to do with "knowing" the man. He should understand that the chances of her taking affirmative action in the future are rather slim. A more honest way for a woman to say this might be, "I don't want to get involved sexually with you at this time. I might feel better about it later, but at this point I do not feel attracted enough to you sexually." Or alternatively, if she does feel attracted to him, but is holding back because of his or her personal situation: "The fact that you are married ... I am married ... you are already paying alimony to three ex-wives makes the situation one that I don't want to get into."

☐ This could be a lead-in to saying, "I don't know you well enough yet to tell you something personal about myself ... to comment on your clothes ... to advise you on that matter." In this case, it may be a sincere and sensible statement or a way of saying, "I don't know you well enough."

"I don't think I really matter to you."

☐ Just what it says. But why was it necessary to say it? What will be accomplished by it? It's a "clutch phrase," which is designed to grab the listener in just the way a drowning person clutches his rescuer.

☐ It's a bid for reassurance, an invitation to: "Of course you matter to me"—and possibly a sign that the relationship is on the skids. Otherwise, no reassurance would be sought.

☐ "I want to know where I stand with you." But why not say just this? It will get better results than the roundabout "I don't think I really matter to you."

☐ Emotional blackmail. It takes a really tough person to answer, "No, you don't matter to me!" So in most cases the relationship will limp along with resentment on one side and insecurity on the other.

"I don't want to talk about it anymore."

☐ "Right now I don't care enough about your feelings to want to talk more. So . . . shut up!"

☐ "What you are talking about makes me so uncomfortable I have to stop the conversation."

☐ "I'm losing control of this interchange so I'll close you off with 'I don't want to talk about it anymore.'" If I succeed at this, I'm also back in control, because I'm saying I don't want to talk now and I'll let you know when or if I'm ever ready to get into this again.

At times this message is the last one said before violence. The receiver of the turn-off feels so frustrated and insulted he/she resorts to something physical to retaliate.

For example, Tom cut his wife off with "I don't want to talk about it anymore," and she responded by stabbing him four or five times in the forearm with a fork. Or, one of the last interchanges between Bill and Gloria before their divorce went this way:

Gloria: I have to talk with you about the marriage. I know you want a divorce from what you said last night, but can't we talk more before you make up your mind?
Bill: I don't want to talk about it anymore.

At this point, Gloria didn't say anything more, but she did go to the stove, took the hot tea kettle and poured the scalding water onto Bill's crotch!

"If you loved me . . ."

☐ This is usually completed by such demands as "you would be more affectionate" or "you would get home earlier" or "you would buy me more clothes" or "you would understand that I have to go bowling with the boys" or "you would spend more time with my parents." This phrase is a clue to a dishonest relationship, in which the speaker is manipulative and maybe even an emotional blackmailer. He connects love with whatever he happens to want the other person to do. "If you loved me" is an attack. If the other person really loves the speaker, it is impossible for him to do enough to prove it. This blackmailing message demands that the receiver give and give and give.

☐ This is a hostile message. The speaker crosses the line into the other person's territory and tells him what his feelings are with "If you loved me. . .". How does the speaker actually know the other person's love feelings?

☐ This can be a martyr message. He's really saying, "If you loved *poor little me*, you would be more affectionate"—or whatever.

> *Direct anger is often the best way to deal with manipulative talk like this. Words such as:*
> *"I really resent your putting it this way."*
> or,
> *"Get off this 'if you loved me' talk."*
> or,
> *"How do you think you come over to me when you talk this way?"*
> or,
> *"I feel like I'm being conned when you talk this way to me."*
> or,
> *"What right have you to tell me if I love you or not. Stay with what you feel and quit trying to read my mind!"*

"*I hate you.*"

☐ Sometimes this has to be said, but the message is almost invariably inaccurate. It would be better to say: "Right now, I hate you." This would be the truth. And there would be fewer hurt feelings and misunderstandings if people understood that such strong emotions are transitory. They may know it, but when they hear "I hate you," the message that comes across is "I always hate you and I always will hate you."

Ironically, sometimes strong words like "I hate you" are healthy signs in a relationship. They testify to the intensity of the relationship. Many couples who never use strong words do not do so because they are indifferent toward each other. There are bound to be occasional conflicts and strong feelings between partners who are close. Couples who keep their relationship alive are open ("up front") with their feelings. They also know how to fight creatively, rather than destructively.

"I know you don't like my mother, but . . ."

☐ This preamble is aimed at conveying understanding of the other person's dislike for "my mother." But rather than understanding, it is really a psychologizing message telling the other person how he/she feels about, in this instance, mother. Psychologizing, whether accurate or not, is always a trespass into the other person. Therefore, rather than conveying understanding, this approach usually puts the other person on guard.

☐ This can easily be a sarcastic message and part of the sarcasm is the psychologizing. "I know you don't like my mother, but you do have some duty to make like you care."

"I look terrible, don't I?"

☐ "Say something nice about me." This is a backhanded (and pretty obvious) way of fishing for a compliment. The word "terrible" sets it up so that something positive is almost bound to be said. The speaker is not so much concerned about the way he looks as about the way he feels—physically or emotionally.

Another way to put it might be, "I don't look my usual self today, do I?" When the question is phrased that way, one leaves the door open to a more honest response, although the burden to issue words of reassurance still rests on the other person.

The straightforward way to find out how one appears to the outside world would be to ask straight out, "How do I look to you today?" This message is not loaded. And if the other person is prepared to be honest, then he can address himself to the realities.

☐ "Do you think there's something wrong with me? How do I look to you—but please don't tell me the truth!" This person does not dare to voice his worries, so he phrases the question in a way that he hopes will help him deny his fears.

"I love you."

☐ It can mean exactly what it says. And that can be wonderful.

☐ It's a test. The speaker wants to find out where he/she stands with the other person. Does he say the words freely and openly out of a feeling of tenderness, cherishing or exuberance? Or does he say them mostly because he expects the other person to say "I love you" back? If the latter is the case then "I love you" is not the real message. Instead the words mean "I want to know where I stand with you."

☐ There would be greater understanding between couples if this message could be correctly interpreted to mean "I love you *right now.*" No one loves another person 100 percent of the time. People's feelings are in a constant flow of change; so no feeling is static or permanent. To add the understanding of "right now" onto the "I love you" message singles the moment out as something special, a time to cherish.

If you feel you have to pay back your partner when you hear the words "I love you," this is a danger signal. Love has become a commodity for barter or reciprocity rather than a gift. If you feel on the spot and feel you have to say "I love you" back, it's a good idea to talk about this feeling at some point. Say how you feel. It might be:
"I feel like you're waiting for me to say 'I love you' right back to you."
    or,
"I feel on the spot."
    or,
"I want to feel free to say 'I love you'; instead, it seems you're hurt if I don't say 'I love you' right back."

"I wish you'd dominate me."

☐ This is an impossible request for anyone to fulfill. If Joan says to John, "I wish . . ." and John proceeds to dominate Joan, he is submitting to her. Therefore, he is not dominating her.

☐ A dishonest message. If it is, and if the other person makes an attempt to be the dominant one in the relationship, the speaker will be furious.

☐ A clue that the speaker is very confused. She (yes, it's usually a female) wants to revert to childhood, does not want to take responsibility, is frightened of decisions. She is asking a man with whom she is romantically or sexually involved to take the place of her daddy or her mommy. Steer clear of such entanglements unless you've always wanted a grown-up child.

Master-slave relationships work well for many couples. It offers great security for both people. But, if the slave decides to become an equal, or if the master gets bored being in charge, a crisis occurs.

Martha was an excellent slave to Ben for the first nine years of marriage. Her greatest rewards came from being able to measure up to Ben's needs. The crisis occurred when the children really didn't need her full-time parenting, and she had time on her hands. By then there was little left of the marriage. Ben took her for granted and found her boring; but she was still an attractive trophy. Fortunately the relationship was not so brittle that it could not survive the transition into an equal adult relationship. It is a delicate transition though. The ex-master has to believe he has more to gain with an equal partner. The ex-slave has to be able to grow to equality without scuttling the partnership with the resentment and hostility which is nearly always part of a shift to an adult-to-adult relationship.

"Let's go to bed."

□ "I want to go to bed. I'm tired. But I don't feel like being alone."

□ "I want to make love, but I'm not sure you do and I don't want to be rebuffed." This usually triggers an exchange that goes along the following lines: "Let's go to bed." (Translation: I feel like making love.) "Let's." (Translation: So do I.)

But if the partner is not in the mood, the exchange, also in code, will probably proceed along these lines: "Let's go to bed." "Oh, I'm not tired. I think I'll stay up and watch the late news." (Translation: I know you want to make love, but I don't feel like it.)

Taken literally this proposal reveals a certain inflexibility. Active sex, to the speaker's mind, is confined to bed. The playful experimental sex play that could take place in different locales such as the sofa, the rug, the shower, the armless rocking chair may be something the speaker is uneasy about—or feels that his partner will not agree to. There is a certain dull conformity to the proposal that may reflect the dull conformity of the sexual act. If this has become your catch phrase for indicating that you feel like sex, it might be time to reconsider. An "I" message would be far more effective, especially a straightforward "I" message like, "I'm feeling really aroused. How would you feel about . . ." and then specify something that you are pretty sure will delight your partner.

"Mother" (instead of "wife" or wife's name); "Father" (instead of "husband" or husband's name)

☐ When these forms are used outside the context of talking to the children, it might indicate that there is very little direct emotional contact between the husband and wife. Their relationship is child-centered and sexual interplay is probably minimal. The wife's main purpose or function to her husband is "Mother" and vice versa.

☐ If used by only one partner, this suggests that the other is the stronger partner and that the speaker is childishly dependent upon him or her. It may be that this partner never completely worked through the process of growing up and still needs a mother or father.

Unless you really like being called "mother" or "father" by your partner, don't let this label stick and become a habit. Such a potent word as "mother" or "father" is more than a casual word. It probably contains a deep emotional charge. Ask yourself whether you really want such an endearment?

"My better half"

☐ Fortunately this oaf-like figure of speech is seldom used anymore. It's a throwback to the time when marriage was considered a unit of one.

☐ Be wary of the person who uses the adjective "better" in the context of a partnership. This is a phony way of trying to speak well of a partner. This phrase is almost always used by the male and indicates a kind of denigration of the wife, a sneer disguised as a compliment.

☐ On a deeper level, the speaker is making a judgment about his partner. Why should that "better" half have chosen the speaker, who has cast himself as the "worse" half? Has she lowered herself? And why? The thrust of this label is insecurity, denigration, and dislike. After all, it is not comfortable for a man (or woman) to be sentenced to go lock-step through life with either a superior or an inferior.

"My wife/husband doesn't understand me."

☐ My wife/husband *should* understand me.

☐ This may contain no hidden meaning; it can be simply a comment about the couple's estrangement.

A frequently believed myth about marriage is that understanding automatically occurs as years are logged into the marriage. Because of this myth, couples often communicate less as the marriage goes on, and yet expect more understanding. This sets up the following kind of unrealistic thinking:
"He should know I'm feeling miserable at this time of the month."
    or,
"She should be sensitive to how I don't want to hear about the problems with the kids as soon as I get home."

Sometimes in my office I ask couples to try the following communication experience. One person interviews the partner as if he doesn't know the individual. What is he/she looking forward to? What disappointments have there been? What makes for most happiness? Is she a day or night person? Then the partners reverse the interviewing. Often couples find that the interviewing, though contrived, helps the relationship.

John, while interviewing Mary, learned to his surprise that she wanted a vacation with him without the kids. Before learning this he had a slow burn going toward Mary, because he felt in competition with the children for Mary's love. He kicked himself for being competitive with his own children, but yet he was. Learning that Mary wanted a vacation with him helped start the marriage on a different track. It became couple centered instead of child centered.

"Right now."

□ These two words should be used more often to clarify messages about feelings. See "I love you" (page 22) and "I hate you" (page 20). One reason some people are so quick to interrupt and get defensive is because they don't get the (usually unspoken) "right now" message. When a person tells you, "I'm angry with you," he translates it as "I'm always angry with you." The incomplete message can result in a drifting apart and eventual separation. We should not expect people to divine that we mean "right now" when we talk about feelings. There are very few mind readers. If more people employed these words when describing their feelings, it would be a step toward clearer communication.

"Tell me that you love me."

☐ The speaker is a loser—and knows it. It's a blackmailing demand that is usually met with counterfeit "money." For instance, John says, "Tell me that you love me," and Joan responds, "Of course I do." How can he be sure she really means it? If she had said, "No, I don't," that would have been too brutal. This demand is like asking for a gift. When the gift is received, it turns out not to be a gift at all, but a payoff.

A better way of phrasing this might be, "I'd like to know where I stand with you, how you feel about me." The other person now does not have to lie for fear the truth would be too brutal. The speaker has given permission to tell the truth. This is an inquiry that can be answered honestly. Also, see page 51 for its use between parent and child.

Some possible responses to this request would be something along the lines of:

"I really feel pressured when you say that to me."

or,

"I do love you, but when you order me to tell you, then I get to feeling stubborn. Since you've started putting me on the spot like this, I find I'm telling you less and less often that I love you. I sure would like to work out something better. How do you feel about that?"

The most pain-filled marriage of all is the one held together by the threat of suicide. It is not so bald as "tell me that you love me or I will kill myself," but it is often, "if you don't give me what I want, and instead leave me, I will kill myself."

One couple sustained a relationship like this for twenty

years. Naturally it did not start for Jim and Jean with the threat of suicide, but within five years the threat and fear of suicide absorbed most of the energy in the relationship. There is never one reason why anything happens in a marriage, but a major reason Jean became suicidal was she found it was almost impossible to get Jim's attention unless she hinted at self-destruction. The trap was set because Jim really believed she might kill herself. In turn, Jean really believed that if she were to do it, his life would be destroyed by the guilt for not keeping her from death.

For years her threats gave her the power to control the relationship. She had the final say on such matters as extent of debt, choice of mutual friends, location of home, and how the children were raised. Suicide was not actually threatened when most decisions were made in the marriage. Jean didn't have to reach for the threat, because Jim believed it was always within her reach.

Finally, when the children were in their late teens, Jim gained the maturity to let Jean know he was no longer responsible for whether she committed suicide. The marriage ended quickly thereafter. Jean did not kill herself at the end of the "survival" marriage. Some years later she married again and the new relationship seemed much happier. She did not have the need to try to control her new husband. Instead she had gained confidence in her capacity to negotiate through to decisions that would fit for both partners.

"We're so happy we never have any arguments/fights/disagreements/conflicts."

☐ This statement does *not* mean that Joan and John, who have enjoyed a long-term relationship, marital or otherwise, are so exquisitely attuned that they live in a state of bliss. It is important to know who's talking. Who is the "we" in this case? Let us say it is Joan. How much is she speaking for herself? And how much for John? One meaning of this statement can be, "I am very happy with John and I like the way we never have any arguments and I think he is happy, too." But John may feel strongly otherwise.

☐ If there are no conflicts in a long-term relationship this is a strong indication that neither Joan nor John cares enough about the other to have a fight. In this case, John is really saying: "We get along okay. We don't bug each other. But I wish I had someone I really cared about and who cared enough about me so we could tell each other how we really feel."

☐ Or Joan may be a dictator in disguise. She is really saying, "I like things the way they are. John does whatever I tell him." The sensitive listener may suspect that submissive John is showing signs of restiveness if Joan feels she has to make this open declaration. John may be ready to mutiny and this long relationship may be on the verge of dissolution.

☐ This may reflect fear of conflict. Neither Joan nor

John dares risk a disagreement. They feel their relationship is based on maintaining a harmonious surface. If this is so, one should think of this as a relationship that is drowning in embalming fluid. Without some "creative conflict," there can be no growth in a relationship.

If both partners want to remain individuals and change and grow at their own speed, then there is bound to be occasional conflict if the relationship is at all close. This is why I use the wording "creative conflict." The main problem in any close relationship is how to be close to the partner yet also free to grow as an individual. These needs conflict and therefore require clear communication and occasional conflict in order to keep the closeness and freedom needs in balance.

"What did you buy that for?"

☐ This may represent the tip of an iceberg of resentment that has been hidden and growing for a long time. The question is designed to put the other person on the defensive.

☐ "I don't like it."

The other person should not answer this question, nor explain why he bought whatever it was. That is falling into a trap that has been set. He should take his cue from the fact that the question was asked at all. An appropriate response would be to say how you feel or ask a return question, such as, "Why do you seem to have such strong feelings about what I bought?" Or, "What do you mean when you ask me that?" These questions should elicit some information about what is really bothering the one who asks the question. Then one can proceed to deal with the real problem.

"Why were you late?"

☐ "I'm angry with you because you're late." This speaker does not want—probably does not *dare*—to let the late one know how angry he is. Asking "why" may provide the angry one with a socially acceptable outlet. If there were no good reason, then the speaker has "permission" to go ahead and vent his anger. If there is a good reason, it may disarm the angry one, unless he is a secret grievance-hoarder. In that case, he will not dare to express anger in the face of an acceptable reason for lateness, but he will suppress the anger and may later blow up over a trivial incident just because of this suppressed simmering anger. It would be better for him to express the anger then and there. It is important that the emotional charge be defused. He might say something like, "Okay, now I understand why you were late and why you couldn't call me, but I was really furious at you when I sat around waiting. I feel better now, but I'm still a little upset."

☐ "Who do you think you are—being late and expecting me to wait for you?" This questioner will soothe his feelings by listening to the latecomer flounder around with an explanation (a wife punishing a husband who stopped for a drink too many after work). This kind of attitude can make even the most plausible excuse seem like an evasion.

□ A simple request for information that shows concern and should not be confused by the tardy one
with the above interpretations. It is not a reproach.

*"Why" questions bypass feelings. The why question asks for
an answer at the thinking or factual rather than the emotional level. If you think there is more to the "why" question
that is coming at you than a request for information, then
respond with how you feel rather than a strictly thinking-
level or factual response. If the question is, "Why were you
late?" then try:*
    *"I resent the way you are talking to me right now. If
you're irritated I wish you'd say it straight out."*

"Will you always love me?"

□ An accurate indication of an infantile person, one
who can be a terrible emotional drag on anyone who
cares about him/her. The speaker does not understand that promises extracted in response to such a
blackmailing kind of question mean very little. This
person is confiding that, "I am so dependent on you
that I won't be able to manage if you stop loving me."
He or she is not mature enough to understand that
love ebbs and flows and may even occasionally disappear for certain periods, but a good relationship can
stand this. Anyone embarking on a serious relationship with such an immature partner should think
hard about the demands of this kind of dependency.

"You never say anything nice to me."

☐ "I feel sorry for myself." The speaker is depressed and feels so inferior that he is reduced to begging the other to tell him something "nice." If the relationship is close, one can never say enough "nice" things to satisfy the chronically depressed or insecure.

☐ The word "never" in this context adds to the desperation of the message.

A word about depression: *If you try to cheer up a depressed person, it may make the depression worse, because an effort to try to get out of the depression can mean additional anger directed inward. This anger is the cause of many depressions. It is as if the depressed person says to himself, "I've got to get hold of myself and pull myself out of this. Look at all I have to be thankful for. It makes me mad at myself that I don't appreciate it more." The most helpful approach for a friend is to talk along with the depressed person as if you were "walking along" beside him. This means addressing yourself to the person's feelings, rather than to his request to "say something nice." It often helps to accept that the other person is depressed and to acknowledge that there are real reasons for him to be that way. For instance:*
    "It sounds as if things are really grim in your business these days."
    or,
    "I've known you now for three years and this situation is just about the worst I've ever heard you talk about."
    or,
    "Sounds like you are really down, and you are feeling even worse because you aren't sure how come."

III

Hidden Meanings Between Parent and Child

*I*t is easy for hidden meanings to become embedded in parent—child communication. This happens because the relationship is not equal, as (hopefully) is the relationship between two adults, particularly close friends or lovers. Instead, the parent—child relationship is lopsided. The power is mostly on the parent's side and the dependency is mostly on the child's side.

Many children learn that they get along better with their parents if they tell them what they think the parents want to hear, rather than what the children are actually feeling and thinking. You can see why it's so easy for a pattern of hidden meanings to develop. For example, think what often happens when a teenage daughter is seeing alot of her boyfriend. In some families the daughter is careful to remain obscure in what she tells the parents: "A group of us went to John's and listened to records." Actually, the daughter went to John's and the two of them drank beer, smoked marijuana, and listened to records.

In other families, when hidden meanings are not the pattern, there is openness and candor in the talk between parents and children. Why is this so?

I believe what has happened is that the parents have learned how to listen to their children. They listen in a way that does not promote hidden meanings. Three books are particularly useful in teaching this listening skill: *Parent Effectiveness Training* by Thomas Gordon, *Between Parent and Child* by Haim Ginott, and *How to Parent* by Fitzhugh Dodson, Los Angeles.

There is a special sadness when hidden meanings become pervasive in parent—child communication. Nearly always the parents mean well and the children want a close and open relationship, but the faulty communication ends up a barrier separating the two generations.

"Ask your mother/Ask your father."

☐ "I'm afraid to say 'no.' I'm too dependent on your approval even though you are the child and I the adult. I'll cop out by telling you to ask your other parent."

☐ "I get mileage out of putting my spouse on the spot. I know he or she feels uncomfortable with what our child wants to do, so I'll make him or her the one who has to say 'no.' "

Example: "Can I have the car?" "Ask your mother." These families indulge in civil wars—one parent trying to put the other down. Parents who relate this way make their family life wearisome and confusing for their children. The children are used as ammunition in the parents' struggle to put pain into each other's lives.

"Be a Man!"

☐ Unless the son is of adult age, this is an impossible demand. It comes over as rejection—and if said with enough intensity, it is scornful rejection.

During counseling work in San Quentin Prison, I knew an inmate who was in for kidnapping and attempted murder. He had been hired for a contract killing. Probably one of the reasons for his crime was many experiences he had with his father during his late teens when he was being taught to "be a man!" The father would take him to a bar and during the drinking, the father would provoke a fight with one of the patrons. The father would then not enter into the fight, but instead force the son to do the fighting. If he didn't fight to the father's satisfaction he would then beat up the son.

☐ "Be more the way I want you to be, for my purposes."

☐ "Stop showing your feelings, particularly tears or feelings of helplessness. Be more like me and submerge most of your feelings . . . keep yourself on 'automatic pilot.' "

Similar destructive demands for "maturity" are "Grow up," "Be an adult," and "Be a lady."

"Be careful."

□ "Be fearful." This is a common parent-to-child message—and a destructive one. It projects onto the child the parent's fearful attitudes. Even when the warning is appropriate, it would be better if phrased as an "I" message. For instance:

"I can't help worrying about your crossing Main Street on the way to school. There's so much traffic."

or,

"I'm worried about your plan to hitchhike alone across the country. I don't think it's safe. I'd feel better if you went with someone."

"Do as you please/Do whatever you want."

□ This can be a loving message that carries a message of trust from a parent to a child. But this use is rare.

□ Usually these words carry a heavy message of indifference, lack of interest. Many permissive parents find out—years too late—that their permissive messages came across to their children as signals of indifference rather than of love, and, because of this, the children grew up feeling insecure.

*"Don't you think your hair is too long . . .
your pants too tight . . . you're wearing
too much make-up . . . you ought to work
harder . . . you're smoking too much . . .
you should go on a diet?"*

☐ This is a hit-and-run message, a way of avoiding the issue while seeming to confront it. "The speaker doesn't say directly what he/she wants. The phoney question can be dismissed with a simple "yes" or "no," disposing of the necessity of following through and taking action. This phraseology is most commonly used by a parent toward a child. A more honest way of handling such concerns would be to say:

"I'm concerned about the length of your hair."
or,
"I'm worried about the amount you smoke . . . or how much weight you're putting on, etc."

This opens the way for an exchange of feelings on the subject.

Efforts by parents to control children on relatively minor issues such as hair length, clothing preference or make-up at times escalate into a ruptured relationship.

Matt's father didn't like his son's shoulder length hair and nagged at him to "get a haircut." The two were at odds for numerous reasons and I believe Matt's choice to keep his hair long served a useful purpose for him. It was one of his few ways to take a stand against his father.

One Saturday morning the father finished his breakfast and snapped at his son, "This is the last time I'm telling you, get a haircut this morning". The son refused. The father grabbed the boy, dragged him into the garage and sheared his hair with scissors. There was a struggle throughout the haircut, hence Matt's hair looked as though he had mange. Matt got the last word on this showdown by keeping his blotchy haircut. This gave him the opportunity to tell whoever asked how he got the "weird" haircut. Following this incident the relationship deteriorated even more. He left home shortly after the haircut, dropped out of high school, moved into an apartment with some other teenagers and paid his way by busing dishes in a restaurant.

One reason Matt's father got into this showdown is because he failed at the most important job of raising a teenager: letting go of the adolescent at the "right" speed, not too quickly, not too slowly.

(If a parent doesn't let go quickly enough there will be unnecessary rebellion by the child. It is ironic, but if a parent succeeds in controlling the teenager too long, child-rearing is a failure, because the child will not grow up to be an individual adult. Have you known a 25 or 30-year-old who hasn't truly left home? The child-rearing process "stalled out." The parents didn't graduate as parents, and the offspring remained children.

"Don't worry. Everything will be all right."

☐ A legitimate message of reassurance from a parent to a child that reflects the parent's greater knowledge and experience. An episode that seems cataclysmic to a child may indeed be nothing more than a passing nuisance. Parents should be careful, however, not to offer false reassurance. Once a child finds that he cannot trust his parent's reassurance, it is difficult to reestablish credibility when being supportive.

"Give me a kiss."

☐ When spoken to a child by a parent, it indicates an unhealthy reversal of roles. If a parent grows increasingly dependent upon a child, either for love or identification, one can look forward to a noisy massive rebellion against the parent sometime during adolescence—much more than the usual adolescent rebellion. It could take the form of direct hostility toward the parent or passive withdrawal from any involvement with the parent or the parent's life, which could in turn trigger an attitude of passivity toward the world at large: school, other people, work, etc. It also acts to frustrate and inhibit a child's natural expressions of affection. The demand for a kiss kills spontaneity.

"How could you say that (or do that) after all I've (we've) done for you?"

☐ The speaker wants to induce guilt. When a parent says this to a child, he often succeeds in inculating guilt. The parent is also working to teach the child not to share his feelings or doings with the parent, but to censor them, because the parent is saying that a balance sheet is being kept on the child's behavior, with mother and father adding up the debits and credits as these are incurred by the child—hardly a loving technique.

□ Sometimes this reflects desperation. If the parent felt confident about his relationship with the child, he would never resort to manipulation of this sort.

□ This is a lever that widens the generation gap. Parents say it to children because children have no ready response. Parents would not be able to get away with saying it to another adult. Parents who hear themselves spouting this line should stop and apologize. It will accomplish nothing constructive. It's too bad that children are too intimidated to ask in return, "What about all I have done for you?" Parents might just remind themselves of the identity, pleasure and satisfaction their children have supplied them— *without* ever asking for an accounting.

When a parent succeeds in making a child feel guilty he always makes the child angry, because deep anger and guilt are inseparable. Seldom is this anger expressed directly. Instead it is left unsaid to smoulder, only to come out at the parent later. In some instances it never comes out at all, but instead becomes a basis for increased estrangement between the parent and the child.

"How many times have I told you not to do that?"

□ An ineffective angry noise. The parent does not expect an answer. What would an answer be? Maybe: "Let me think, I guess you told me not to do it forty-two times?" If a parent wants to communicate displeasure effectively it is better to say, "I'm really angry at you for doing that."

"I'd be careful if I were you."

☐ This destroys the possibility of openly discussing a hazard (if it actually exists). The phrase assumes that the person to whom this remark is directed is in fact interested in hearing what the speaker would do if he/she were in the "endangered" person's situation. Only seldom does the "endangered" person feel that the speaker's experience qualifies him to advise. If he wanted advice he would ask for it.

☐ If a parent is really worried about a course of action proposed by another person, he should express his concern directly and not presume to put himself in the other's place—or pretend that he can experience the other's feelings.

☐ This can be a threat, plain and simple. An "or else" ultimatum is implied.

☐ When this phrase is tossed at children, particularly teen-agers who are struggling to gain an individuality of their own, this presents a challenge. The chances that an adolescent would heed this message and would actually be careful are practically nil.

"I forbid you to do that."

☐ This is dangerous talk. Can the speaker back it up? And if he can, what would happen then? Parents often maneuver themselves into confrontations that produce such prohibitions as, "I forbid you to see Johnny," or "I forbid you to smoke." It's just about impossible to enforce these dictatorial demands, so neither the parent nor the child can win and resentments deepen. One of the most important rules about child rearing is, "Don't have showdowns that you can't win. If you can't win them, avoid them."

☐ This can be a challenge. To be told not to do something works on the other person as a provocation and increases the chances that he will do the "forbidden" act.

Often couples get married not for any redeeming reason, but because the parents said, "I forbid you to go out with Johnny." If the daughter has a big enough need to claim her individuality from her parents, this can bring forth a powerful, unconscious attraction to Johnny and, in some instances, marriage.

"If you want to."

☐ This is often a healthy message from a parent to a child. Much better than "Be careful" or "Why do you want to do that?" or "Do as you please." This phrase helps a child learn to be aware of what he or she really wants. Learning to figure out what one wants is one way to interpret one's own emotions and to understand what triggers one's most basic feelings.

"I wouldn't do that if I were you."

☐ This is often a flat-out threat with an undisguised

promise of retaliation. "If I were you" carries an ominous ring, and is also presumptuous. A clearer way of saying what the speaker usually means would be: "I feel angry when you do that."

□ This can be an arrogant trespass into another's personal space. The speaker is saying, "What I would do is what you should do. And what I wouldn't do is what you shouldn't do."

"Just a minute."

□ "Just a minute" is a great passive resistance from child to parent or vice versa. If the resentment beneath the passive resistance is not dealt with, the relationship will become clogged.

□ When a parent uses this phrase to a child, it is almost always dishonest. The child will take it to mean that in sixty seconds his mother or father will be prepared to attend to his question or problem. To the parent, the phrase probably means:
"I'm busy right now. I'll be with you shortly."
or possibly,
"Stop pestering me. I'll be there in five minutes."
Both of these are clearer messages than "Just a minute."

"Let's not talk about this anymore for the moment."

☐ Watch out for that innocuous-sounding little phrase "let's." The speaker probably does not want to take responsibility for postponing an unpleasant talk or terminating a discussion that is not going his way, so he makes the other person share in his negative decision by using "let's." This is a trespass on the other's personality. It is supposed to force him to adopt the same view or position as the speaker. Parents often use this phrase with children, not realizing that it is almost always self-defeating. An adult can perhaps be intimidated into agreeing with a manipulator who prefaces an order with "let's," but children, particularly teen-agers, regard this phrase as a challenge. Their instinctive reaction is to assert themselves, to show that they are separate personalities. In these cases, the phrase works to put distance between parent and child.

An "I" message is much superior to a "let's" message. Example:
  "I don't want to talk about this anymore right now."
  or,
  "I don't want to talk about this anymore for the moment, but I'll do it after dinner if you want."
  It is essential that children get a model from their parents for communicating with "I" messages. In this way the children will learn to talk openly and directly with their feelings when it is appropriate to do so.

"My parents don't understand me."

☐ Who says they should? Parents are not super-human.

☐ This may mean: "My parents don't love me." It usually indicates a confusion between love and agreement on the part of the child. When his parents don't see eye to eye with him, he interprets this as lack of love. For instance, "If my parents would let me smoke marijuana in my bedroom," says a sixteen-year-old, "then they'd understand where I'm really at." Such statements reveal that the speaker does not understand the strength of the love that it takes to protect a youngster from himself.

☐ When used by an adult, this is usually an indication that the speaker has not yet resolved his relationship with his parents and is still childishly dependent upon them. When a situation arises in which he and his parents do not absolutely agree, he reverts to the childish complaint that, "My parents don't (or didn't) understand me." It would be far better to say to one-self, "Well, they did the best they could." If one feels they made mistakes (and what parents haven't?) forgive them, and go on from there. But words are cheap; forgiving a parent may not be possible. Psychotherapy then can be a useful tool for gaining freedom from a parent.

Adults who hold on to anger against their parents are not allowing themselves to grow. The anger can be an enormous energy drain as well as a contamination of their potential to be a free person. Example: the loss of freedom that is felt when one says, "I don't like him because he reminds me of my father," or "I should do well because my father expected that of me."

"Stop that. You make me nervous."

□ The speaker is usually the mother who is being driven out of her wits by squabbling children, a noisy record player, a dangerous balancing act, etc. She is expressing her feelings—possibly understating them—quite straightforwardly, but there is a hidden meaning here that children pick up. And that is "Stop that. I cannot maintain control of myself when you do that." This confers a frightening power on the child. He or she realizes that he/she can control his/her mother's feelings. Spoiled children thrive on this power. They intuitively know how to make the mother react with nervousness, anger, or helplessness.

A parent would be better advised to say:

"That music is really getting to me. Could you turn it down?"

or,

"I can't stand this fighting, if it goes on for one more minute, each one of you will have to go to your room or go outdoors."

In these examples the mother is "owning" her own feelings, and reporting them, then saying what she wants done. If she only reports her feelings or only says what she wants done the message is incomplete and the relationship will suffer.

"Tell me that you love me."

☐ If a child says to a parent, "Tell me that you love me," this should be considered a warning signal. It is time for a talk—and about many things other than love, too. The parent should try to be extremely perceptive and sensitive when he hears this. A six-year-old might be really saying, "Stay and talk to me a little before you turn off the light and say 'good night.' I'm scared of the dark." Or the child may have done something that he thinks is wrong and wants reassurance before confessing to it. Or it could be nothing more than a manipulative stall in the same vein as "I'm thirsty" or "I have to go to the bathroom"—those classic techniques employed to delay being left alone to go to sleep. Active listening will pay off here.

☐ When a parent says this to a child, it is a message of reversed dependence, an indication that the parent and child have changed roles. The parent is too needy of the child's love. This gives the child too much power.

"We'll see."

☐ "No, I don't want you to do it."

☐ "I can't make up my mind right now." If true, it would be wiser to say it just this way. This is an honest answer. It would be more open—and more courteous to the child—to add something like:
    "It depends on how much it will cost."
    or,

"It depends on what other plans we have for that weekend."

This is a typical parent-to-child response and labels the adult as someone who does not have the directness to come straight out and say "No" when he means it. Very soon the child understands exactly what the vague "We'll see" means and also understands the evasive maneuvering of the adult. A better response would be to say:
"No, I think you're too young to do that."
or,
"It costs too much."
or,
"I don't approve of that."

"When I was your age . . ."

☐ Who are you kidding? You never were his or her age, at least not in your child's eyes! No child can switch perspectives as this phrase demands. Also, different eras turn chronological ages into different experiences—or into the same experiences but experienced in a totally different way. This is almost always a prelude to a preachy message. It tends to produce instant deafness in a child or adolescent. If you hear yourself starting out this way, apologize.

"WHY DON'T YOU . . ." MESSAGES

☐ These are usually communication blockers. The phrase is a put-off, a distancer. It's hostile. It puts the other person on the defensive. It usually gets no action but often increases resentments between generations. Examples:
"Why don't you get up earlier?"
"Why don't you write the book report?"
"Why don't you pick up your room?"
"Why don't you wash the car?"

☐ None of these messages makes the listener feel better about himself—or about the speaker. The tone is critical. It is rarely possible to come up with sensible answers to these "questions." They are really not questions but criticisms, or sometimes commands. The speaker doesn't really want to know why you don't—and the listener usually senses this.

If the listener takes the "Why don't you" message literally, then he must explain why he will or won't do whatever it is. Because of the use of this phrase, the child is immediately put on the defensive, in a one-down position. Repeated instances of this make it difficult and sometimes impossible for a young person to develop a healthy self-esteem.

☐ "Why don't you" messages are not only crippling but malignant when beamed toward children, because parents have the power to punish noncompliance.
"Why don't you comb your hair?" "Why don't you sit up straight?" "Why don't you go do your homework?" These are not requests for information.

They are commands: "Comb your hair." "Sit up straight." "Do your homework."

These "Why don't you's" mask a parent's insecurity, the usually justified feeling that control over the child is slipping out of the parent's hands. The parent is afraid of losing the child's love if he tells him to do as he is told, so he phrases his command as a "Why don't you" to save face and avoid a showdown.

"You" MESSAGES

☐ The "You" message is usually aggressive and intrusive. It may be concealed behind a facade of sanctimoniousness. For instance, "You should not litter," or "You should stop writing those dirty words on the wall." Listen to the messages in: "You should stop smoking." "You ought to get married." "You ought *not* to get married. You're too young." They are all very high-handed communications—and largely ineffective. Some people will simply shrug off the "You" message. Others, especially young people, will view it as a challenge. In this case, they go ahead and get married or keep on smoking, although in their heart of hearts they know they are too young and that smoking is bad for their health. But they are not going to be put in the position of knuckling under to the issuer of the "You" message.

☐ The person interested in open communications will try to cut "You" messages out of all his conversation with young and old alike. These messages are undesirable, unrewarding, hostility-provoking—and worst of all they tend to stifle communication. The "You" message shows the user as a person who does not want to come to grips with a problem. If he did, he would turn it into a straightforward "I" message. For instance:

"I wish you didn't smoke. I worry about your health, especially when I hear you coughing."
or,
"I know you love David very much. He's certainly a fine young man. But I love you and I really wish you two would postpone marriage for a year or so. I can

understand that you have a beautiful relationship, but
I have seen so many young marriages that have
turned into traps that I worry. I want you to be as
happy as possible."

Neither of these messages may convince the
young person to change, but neither will they shut
down communication because they convey a sense of
caring rather than judging.

"You shouldn't do that."

☐ "I don't want you to do that." Such an alternative
"I" message is more honest and would have more
effect because the parent is expressing an opinion,
not trying to control the child by saying what he/she
should or shouldn't do. Children can hear and respond to opinions better than "should" talk.

*It is interesting to note how many of these "you shoulds/
shouldn'ts" are addressed by parents to children. In fact, they
are most often only said to children and seldom, used by an
adult to another adult. Parents who talk this way often regard their children as possessions that they have the right to
own. This attitude produces a pattern of communication that
is distinctive and also destructive to both parent and child.*

IV

Hidden Meanings Between Friends

*F*riendships offer the best opportunity for learning to talk openly and directly instead of hiding behind camouflaged meanings. The opportunity is greater between friends than between lovers, parents and children or between mere acquaintances, because a friendship gives you the greatest freedom of choice. You begin the relationship at will; you can deepen it at will or end it at will. No similar degree of freedom exists within the bonds of love or marriage or between parent and child.

This freedom provided by friendship is one of the reasons why many people find their richest relationship is with a friend rather than a spouse. It is paradoxical but true: the freedom of friends to move away from each other is one of the reasons for the closeness that can develop between them.

"Are you tired . . . angry . . . worried?"

☐ "I'm exasperated with you." Such seemingly solicitous inquiries may reveal the speaker's frustration at not being able to get the attention of the listener. There's a sense here of "What's wrong with you, anyway?"

☐ An "inside out" question. The speaker feels "tired . . . worried . . . angry, etc.," but isn't willing to admit it. This may be because he is trying to convince himself that it is all right to feel tired (or whatever), so he asks the other person to check out whether his feeling is appropriate.

☐ This may be an authentic question to find out what is going on inside the other person. If so, it is important that the question "Are you tired?" express real concern, because the direct question "Are you tired? . . . angry? . . . worried?" asks the other person to open up and share what he is feeling.

"Are you trying to tell me that I should work harder . . . have bad breath . . . am boring?"

☐ This usually reflects hurt. It's seldom used to clarify a positive statement like, "Are you trying to tell me that I have a beautiful figure . . . that I won the golf tournament . . . that my book made the Japanese best-seller list?" The speaker is conveying a message of distress. "What you are saying hurts me so much that I have tried to translate it for myself by saying, 'Are you trying to tell me. . . .' " This is a protective mechanism. There's an angry edge to the phrase that makes it easier to bear the hurt.

☐ It could be a request for further clarification. "You may know what you're saying, but you're not making yourself clear to me. If you mean I should work harder, just what is it you want me to do?" Or, "When you say that you'd like to take your vacation alone this year, are you trying to tell me that our friendship is over?"

"Ask yourself, 'What can I learn from this experience?' "

☐ This is sermonizing; and it is seldom appropriate, useful or even bearable. A sensitive person doesn't hand out such self-righteous advice when another is in pain. There's a sense here of gloating superiority.

If the friendship means enough to you, why not let the speaker know how this message comes over to you. For example: "You know, you aren't being very helpful. Sounds like you want to explain a lesson in life to me, but I'm not very open to that right now."

"Don't be defensive" or "Don't be so defensive."

☐ The speaker has the other person tied up in knots

with this one—and that's just what he wants. If the
other replies, "I'm not on the defensive," the fact of
answering it is an admission that he feels attacked. So
he actually *is* on the defensive. If the other person
truly were feeling and acting defensive, this message
would be no help. It just puts him in a worse position.

☐ This phrase is a nasty attack, and falls into the
category of psychologizing hence telling the other
person what he/she is feeling. It's a trespass into the
other person's territory.

*If you care to put the energy into the relationship, a useful
response here is to express your feelings about the attack.*
    "I really resent you when you tell me how I'm feeling."
    or,
    *"Don't tell me I'm defensive—I really don't like the way
you act as if you can read my emotions. You don't know what
I'm feeling!"*

"Don't be discouraged."

☐ This can be a helping message. The speaker is conveying support, if the underlying message is: "I am
with you. I have confidence in you. If you keep on as
you are, I believe everything will turn out all right." It
would be preferable if the speaker did not stop with a
brief "Don't be discouraged," but went on to convey
his support.

☐ Sometimes this is used as a conversation stopper. The speaker can't stand hearing about the other's discouragement. He is too fragile to expose himself to others' problems.

☐ This is one of the most frequent "rescue messages." To rescue without also patronizing or insulting the other person is a delicate effort and requires clear and open give-and-take.

☐ "I wish I could be helpful and bolster you up. That's what I'm trying to say." And if the speaker would put it this way, it would be even more helpful. There would be no chance for the other to interpret it as a brush-off.

"Don't be ridiculous."

☐ "You *are* ridiculous" is what this means. Such an insulting admonition sometimes triggers an equally hostile reply. For instance, "What do you mean? Ridiculous?" This often sets off a back-and-forth of recriminations.

☐ The speaker is obviously scornful of the other person, but more than that he reveals himself as thinking he has the right to judge others. This is a clue to pomposity, impatience—and sometimes an underlying insecurity that makes him have a need to put others down.

*"Don't cry. Nothing is worth getting
that upset about." or "Nothing is
worth crying about."*

☐ This phrase is absolutely insensitive. The speaker
may find nothing in life important enough to warrant
tears, but that does not mean that others share his
insensitivity. An appropriate reaction to this statement would be to cross the speaker off one's list of
people with whom one can share sorrows—or joys.
The person who uses this phrase is also liable to point
out the flaws in happy events and take the edge off
another's joy.

"Don't worry."

☐ This is an attempt to be helpful and supportive, but
an ineffectual one. The speaker is really saying, "I
can't help you on this matter you're worrying about,
so I'm telling you not to worry. That way, I feel better,
because it makes me uncomfortable to see you so obviously distressed." This raises a question: Is it better
to keep one's worries to oneself? In some cases, yes.
Some people are so fragile that they are shaken by
another's worries, not because they empathize with
the worries, but because they feel threatened themselves.

☐ It is a naive message. According to this, worry can
be switched on and off like a light. If one is to stop
worrying, something constructive must be substituted
for the worry. If one simply stops, a vacuum is

created, then the worry comes flooding right back. This supposedly comforting phrase actually establishes distance between people rather than bringing them closer together or making a sympathetic connection between them.

"Don't worry. Everything will be all right."

☐ This can be a legitimate message of reassurance between adults. For instance between a doctor and patient or a lawyer and client.

☐ This can also be an annoyed and frustrated message between friends. For instance: "I wish you'd stop talking about your problems. I'm sympathetic, but there's nothing I can do to help you. And besides, I think you're making a mountain out of a molehill." If a friend wanted to be honestly and lovingly helpful, he might say something like "I wish you didn't have to suffer through this. I know it's hard. I wish I could help you. But all I can say is that in my experience the time comes when such an episode is finally forgotten, or the problem solved, or one finds one can live with it." This kind of message, instead of offering cheap reassurance, shows concern, introduces another perspective and is more palatable to the person who is suffering.

☐ Sometimes people who say this are indulging in a form of prayer. They are praying and hoping that what they say is correct. They are trying to bolster their own very shaky confidence. And on another level they are pleading, "Please, for God's sake, don't go to pieces. Don't cry. Don't despair. I can't stand it. If you let go, I may let go, too. So, don't worry. At least not out loud."

☐ In some cases this reflects tenderness and support and is not necessarily to be taken at its superficial meaning. For instance, John tells Joan: "I got fired today. But don't worry," he adds. "Everything will be all right. I'm sure I'll find something else very quickly." Joan hugs him and says, "I'm sure you will." And then she in turn says, "Don't worry. Everything will be all right."

The translation of Joan's message is "I know how you feel. I know what a blow it is for you. And I suspect that it will take quite a time to find another job that's as good. But don't worry. I'm strong. I'm not going to go to pieces. We'll see this through together."

However, it would be even more reassuring if Joan were to spell it out in these words instead of expecting John to decode her brief, tender message.

☐ Some people use this phrase to signal that they want to avoid deep feelings because they are not comfortable with them. They prefer to be superficial so that there is no danger that they will become involved with another person.

"Do you think I talk too much?"

☐ "If I do, please don't tell me. That's not the answer I want to hear."

□ It's possible, but unlikely, that the questioner really wants to know.

"I am only a woman."

There's a lot of tangled-up emotion packed into this little sentence:

□ The speaker feels that women are inferior to men.

□ She wants pity.

□ She wants something else, too. She would not use this phrase except as an introduction to a demand (often concealed) for power, attention, support, etc. And when it is presented in such a self-abnegating way, it might be more difficult to refuse.

"I can't help myself."

□ This can be a pathetic cry for help, so listen carefully. He may be saying, "I am helpless. Somebody please help me. I am pushed around by forces beyond my control."

□ Humorous overstatement that implies acceptance of oneself. For instance, it could mean, "I know I eat too much and I can't help myself, but when I say this I don't *really* mean that I can't help myself. All I mean is that I'm having a real struggle with myself in trying to control my eating."

"I can't stay on a diet."

☐ This is, quite simply, the truth. The speaker is really saying, "I am out of control when it comes to eating." This person can often help himself or be helped by a better understanding of what the word "diet" means to him. "Diet" to many people means "jail," "confinement," "deprivation," "pain." All these meanings carry with them a kind of unavoidable rebellion. The person wants to break out of jail, break free of the tyranny of the word "diet." Sometimes these people can come to terms with the necessity for eating less by learning to distinguish between appetite and hunger. Hunger is authentic. The body signals it needs food. Appetite is a yearning for a particular food, an eclair, a cookie, candy. If the person learns to say "no" to appetite and eat only when hunger is operating, he will have a good chance of losing weight. Appetite messages will disappear if one can wait them out.

☐ A cop-out. The speaker is refusing to take responsibility for his own actions. It is a return to infantilism. The implication is that "I have a war going on inside me. Part of me is the dieter—and part is the gorger. When they collide the gorger wins." This person is asking for you to involve yourself in his life. But if you should, he will always find reasons why he "can't stay on a diet." This kind of person feels best when he has a number of people upset about his problems—and all the time he refuses to do anything to resolve them.

"I hate to say I told you so, but . . . . ."

□ Then why say it!

□ This is a set up that is supposed to make the recipient less resistant to whatever the message. "I hate to say I told you, but you should have gotten the flu shot," or "used birth control," or "gotten the brakes fixed."

□ "I hate to say I told you so," is a phoney message and the "flu shot," "birth control," or "brake" message that follows probably has basically a hostile motivation. If there isn't hostility, then why would it be said in this way in the first place?

"I have to tell you . . ."

□ "I want to butter you up by making you believe that you are so important to me (or have so much power over me) that I must tell you this."

□ When it's a matter of gossip, the speaker means, "I can't restrain myself. I have to tell you. I get my kicks from being the first one to pass on some juicy tidbit."

□ In a situation where the relationship between two people has deteriorated or is mixed up in some way, this may be a straightforward effort to clear things up.

☐ It can be a nasty, hurtful attack as in "I have to tell you that you're the least popular person in the office." Why does he have to tell you? The speaker who presents unpleasant news prefaced by this phrase gives himself away as one who relishes his task. He likes hurting others.

Frequently a useful response to this "I have to tell you" message is: "Why are you telling me this?" This confronts the other person with what he is doing. It also lets him know that you won't join in with the speaker by passively listening.

"I haven't any self-discipline."

☐ "I'll tell you how awful I am. And in return you had better tell me that I am wrong." Such an overstatement is a form of game playing. It is manipulative, a way to get the other person to say, "Don't be so hard on yourself."

☐ In some instances this is not a ploy to get support, but a statement of fact: "I haven't any self-discipline."

"I know how you feel."

☐ This is presumptuous and ignorant. No one knows how another feels. They can only guess, and the usual guess is that they feel the way the speaker would feel under such circumstances. The only way to know how another feels is to ask him—and even then there may be difficulty in transmitting feelings.

□ No matter how it is used, it's a turnoff. It puts an end to talk. If the speaker announces—no matter how sympathetically—that he knows how the other feels, he prevents the other from talking about his feelings. So, while this seems full of goodwill and understanding on the surface, it leads to misunderstanding and puts distance between speaker and listener.

□ This can be encouragement to someone who is having trouble talking.

"I know what you mean."

□ It could be heartfelt empathy: "I've been through that same experience and I know exactly what you're talking about."

□ Or it may be patronizing, a verbal pat on the head; "Yes, yes, I know what you mean. I'm rather surprised you find it worth mentioning."

□ It might indicate boredom: "I know what you mean. Now shut up."

□ Or it could reveal impatience: "I get your point and I wish you would go on to the next point."

"If I were you . . ."

□ The person saying this thinks he knows what is best for you. This point of view is intrusive and bound to reduce the possibility of real communication.

☐ This is one of the worst lead-ins for uninvited advice. Almost any message to follow will come over as preaching.

If you want to give advice to a friend or loved one, it will help to first get an agreement that the other person wants your advice. It could go like this:
    "I've been thinking about the struggle you've been having over your work. Want some ideas?" "Yes. That might be helpful." Then follow with the advice.

    Compare this approach with, "If I were you, I'd get out of sales work."

"I'm so busy I don't have time to think."

☐ This could reflect the exact state of affairs. John is so involved with an important project that he has no time for anything else. He exaggerates slightly to make his point.

☐ It could reveal hostility and evasion. Anne's husband is out of town on business three weeks out of four, which means that she has to handle the family budget, cope with the children and manage the house by herself. This month the checking account is overdrawn. Her husband asks how this happened. Anne says, "I'm so busy . . . etc. You're never home. I have to take the responsibility for everything." What she really means is, "I know I was careless, but I'm trying to avoid all the responsibility you've dumped on me. You're leaving me in the lurch, making me attend to your share of the family responsibilities as well as mine."

☐ It may mean fear and insecurity. John was promoted to a job that is really too much for him. He was asked to draw up a traffic plan. His boss asks him when he can expect to have the plan on his desk. John gestures at his overflowing *In* box and exclaims, "I'm so busy . . . etc." What he really means is, "I don't think I'm experienced enough to work out that complicated traffic plan. I've let myself in for a lot of routine paperwork so that my boss will think that I'm too busy to do the plan and maybe he'll ask someone else to do it. Better that than let him find out I can't handle it."

☐ It can indicate fear. Anne complains she's bored. Her husband suggests she takes some courses. She responds, "I'm so busy . . . etc. How could I possibly find time to go to class and study?" She is really saying, "I can avoid developing my mind and my emotions by keeping myself so busy that it is out of the question for me to develop my potential. Besides, how do I know what my husband might be doing while I am in class? I'd rather complain and have people feel sorry for me."

"I'm sorry I'm late."

☐ This is a direct and appropriate statement of regret.

☐ It can also be a perfunctory, *pro forma* apology that

means, "I am so important you have to wait for me. My time is more valuable than yours."

☐ It is also sometimes a way of getting off the hook and not allowing the other person to express justified anger or resentment over being kept waiting. People who use it this way tend to think they can get away with almost anything as long as they say "I'm sorry." It's a sign of immaturity, of the child inside the adult shell who still thinks the world revolves around him.

☐ "I'm not trying to cover for being late; I'm just afraid of your anger, and I hope my saying 'I'm sorry' will reduce your strong feelings."

"I should cut down on (or stop) my drinking."

☐ This is a trial balloon. This person really is asking, "I should stop drinking, shouldn't I?" Or, "Do you think I should stop drinking?" His use of the word "should" indicates ambivalence. So, at a deeper level, he is saying, "I'm flirting with the idea of stopping my drinking." Or at bottom, his real meaning is probably, "I think I'm drinking too much, but I have no intention of stopping—although I know it would be a good idea." In this last level, the speaker acts as an alter ego to himself. This reflects deep conflict between what he thinks is good for him and what he is able to do.

A sensible response would be: "I'm not sure what you mean when you say that." If the sentence were "I want to cut down *(or stop) drinking,"* then it would be clearer what the speaker meant because it is easier to understand "want" messages than "should" messages.*

"I shouldn't tell you this, but . . ."

☐ "I want to be closer to you." This is a way of trying to establish an intimate relationship with another person, by making him someone special with whom the speaker can be indiscreet. It can be an indirect, sincere compliment to the effect that "I know I can trust you. You are more discreet than I am."

☐ Watch out. If he shouldn't tell you, why is he telling you? Is he trying to con you? Is he trying to start trouble? If he uses a phrase like, "I shouldn't tell you, but I understand that John's wife is running around with another man . . . that the boss is a homosexual . . . that your doctor was sued for malpractice," he may be trying to turn you into a cat's paw, someone who will repeat gossip for him.

"I wouldn't lie to you."

☐ Yes, he would. The speaker protests too much and by his very protestation underlines that he has a choice of lying or not lying. The listener should be doubly on guard. If the speaker is not lying at the moment, he has revealed that he might—and probably will—lie at other times in the relationship.

"Just think of all the things you have to be thankful for."

☐ This is paternal talk and seldom appropriate. Who would want to hear this sort of message? It is usually said in response to hearing about something that is making the other person uncomfortable. The speaker tries to buck him up by saying, "Look what you've got to be thankful for." But it doesn't help. All it does is put distance between the two people—and at a time when one of them could use some evidence of caring. A more appropriate message would be, "I really don't know what to say. I wish I could be helpful to you." That, at least, indicates some understanding of how upset the other is and does not dismiss his feelings or the situation.

"Nobody understands me."

☐ "People don't think the way I want them to think." This kind of reaction is like putting oneself in jail. It narrows the possibility of meaningful contact and communication with others. The speaker, quite unconsciously, is revealing that he is not capable of having an understanding with someone with whom he may disagree on a few (or many) issues. He does not understand the stimulation and growth possible when two sincere people argue diametrically different points of view.

☐ "Feel sorry for me. I'm all alone in the world." This childish plea for sympathy is used most often by persons who are not willing to make the effort to understand others. The speaker betrays a childlike belief in his own wisdom and omnipotence. He cannot entertain the idea that there are other ways of looking at the world than his. His willful arrogance betrays weakness and immaturity.

"She's a hell of a lay!"

□ The essence of male chauvinism. The word "lay" debases intercourse to a "body trip." The fact that the speaker is discussing his sexual experience with someone else is another indication that he considers women (or this woman) simply as convenient objects and uses them as a cigarette smoker (male) uses an ash tray (female)—as a receptacle.

"Shrink"

□ Possibly the person who refers to his therapist as a "shrink" should think seriously about his relationship to the therapist. This word can indicate that the person feels he is being diminished by treatment, that his personality is being shrunk because of all the introspection, abstracting and analysis. "Why did I do that? Because my mother did this or that? And what does that mean to me now?"

For some people, therapy can be likened to the process that turns a plum into a prune, rather than the reverse. Many people go through psychotherapy and come out of it less in touch with themselves than they were before they began. They become blunted and often drearily narcissistic.

☐ Therapy can generate dependency on the therapist, and dependency often makes for hostility. The label "shrink" can be one way of venting this hostility.

☐ Can be a label of endearment.

"Tell me the truth."

☐ This is hostile. It starts off by stating that the other is not telling the truth. There is an edge of anger here, and the anger will reduce the chance of getting the truth. A better way of putting it would be, "I want you to level with me on this."

☐ It could indicate apprehension. The speaker fears that the other is holding back some bad news. The doctor has not given him all the facts. For instance, what is usually meant is: "No matter how bad the news is, I can handle it. And I'd rather know everything than be left to imagine the worst, so tell me the truth." And he would be better off by amplifying the message in just this way.

☐ It is insulting—and naive, as if one could command the truth. The speaker implies that if he did not insist on the truth, he would get some sort of substitute for the truth or a shading of the truth.

You may want to pick up on the implication of this message that you might not tell the truth. Words like this would do it: "You know, when you say, 'Tell me the truth,' I hear it as suggesting I might not. I want you to know I will tell the truth!"

"Things will get better."

□ This is a meaningless noise that can be hurtful because it is so superficial. How does anyone know if things will get better for someone else? They don't know. The message is: "I don't want to hear about your problems. They will upset me and remind me that I, too, can suffer." A better way of putting this message, a way that conveys caring and sincerity, would be, "I hope things get better for you."

"We don't have much in common."

□ This is used by work or status oriented people who tend to suppress or ignore their feelings. The result is they really don't know whether or not they like or dislike the other person. They judge relationships entirely by what they have in common. "We don't have much in common" is their way of ending a relationship—a business one, a social one, particularly a sexual or "love" relationship. These people place emphasis on "having something in common" (rather than on feelings of warmth, attraction, empathy) because they are not in touch with their own feelings.

□ Or this might mean just what it says, "We don't

connect on much, because I don't think I have much
in common with him."

"What are you doing tonight?"

□ Here we have one of the most familiar of manipulative statements. It may derive from a one-down
position, such as: "What are you doing tonight?"
"Nothing." "Can I come over and see you?"

The speaker ends up by asking permission. A
good response to this ploy is, "I'm not sure. It depends. Why do you ask?" This forces the speaker to
do what he should have done in the first place—come
out directly with whatever was on his mind.

From a one-up position, it goes this way: "What
are you doing tonight?" "Nothing." "I wonder if
you'd like to go to the movies."

In this case, the speaker has set it up so the other
has to admit that he has nothing on for the evening.
Therefore, when he (or more usually she) is asked to
go to the movies, she should be properly humble and
appreciative.

A better way by far would be to say, "If you're not
busy tonight, how about going to the movies? They're
playing such and such." This is direct, states that you
would like the other's company and outlines your
plans for the evening.

"What does he see in her?"

□ "I'm jealous." There is also an underlying meaning
of "How could he be attracted to her when I'm right
here?"

☐ "I don't like her." But she doesn't want to be this frank so she turns it around to ask how he can possibly like that woman.

☐ It could mean either one of the above—or both—with an additional twist of "I don't want to let people know how I feel about her, so I attempt to conceal my feelings behind a question." Unfortunately, the jealousy and dislike are so strong, they come right through this transparent question.

"Why aren't you (can't you be) more spontaneous?"

☐ The speaker does not want the other to be more spontaneous. The point of this question is to make the listener feel inadequate. If the aim were really to help the other be more spontaneous, the speaker would do better to try to help the listener express himself less self-consciously. And since this particular question is one of the most inhibiting he could have settled on, he won't accomplish his aim this way.

☐ A better way to help another achieve spontaneity would be to phrase the question along the lines of "I wish you could be a little more open with your feelings. I'm quite often baffled as to what you're thinking or feeling." This kind of message, which is first of all an "I" message, is an indication of caring. It shows that the speaker wants to know more about the other person and that he is suggesting it would be helpful if his feelings could show more transparently on the outside—in his face, in the way he talks, in his gestures—and finally, in his words.

*"Why do you have such a need to
compete/interrupt/gossip/go into debt/be
late/pick a fight/buy clothes, etc.?"*

☐ Analyze the context here, since this is one of those
either/or situations: either goodwill or hostility.

☐ It may indicate sincere interest, a desire to know
just what drives the other person to these uncomfortable behaviors. In that case, it carries an additional
meaning. John is really telling Mary, "I get tense
when I talk to you because I believe you're going to
interrupt me. It changes the quality of my feeling
toward you." Or he might be saying, "I really like you,
but whenever we're together, you seem to seize on
any excuse to pick a fight. What is it that sets you off?"
This question can indicate tenderness and caring.

☐ It can also be a hostile message. When Mary asks
John, "Why do you always need to be late?" she is
putting him down on two counts. First, the use of the
word "need" implies that John cannot control his
chronic tardiness, that he is out of control. Second,
the very question hints that Mary knows what John's
psychological needs are better than he does. She is
one-upping him.

*Rather than respond to the "why" question, it would be more
effective to respond with what you feel. For instance: "I
really feel on guard when you put the question this way. How
do you know I have a particular need?"*

"Why do you want to do that?"

This question and others such as "Why do you want to move?" "Why do you want to have a baby?" or "Why do you feel that way?" reveal little of what the speaker is feeling, and because of this are difficult for open communication.

☐ This is not truly a question, but a way of opposing what the other person is saying. But instead of saying "I," the speaker hides behind "Why?" He might really mean, "I think you're crazy to want to move," or "With all your talk about zero population what do you mean have another child!" or "You shouldn't feel that way."

The "Why?" used this way is a form of bait. If you go for the bait, you have to explain or justify yourself. Rather than responding to the "Why?" by explaining yourself, how about, at times, asking "Why do you ask the question?"

☐ This can be a genuine request to know more, but "Why?" seldom succeeds at finding out more. For reasons why this is so, go on to the following paragraphs headed "Why" messages.

"Why" messages

Most questions beginning with "why" tend to close down communication rather than foster openness and directness. The response to a "why" question is often a defense or justification. Compare:

"Why do you feel that way?" "I don't know, I just do."

with

"I wish you would tell me more of how you feel about this."

This message is an invitation. The "Why" message is a challenge. The questioner puts the other person into the position of reporting *up* to him. One reason for this is that the person asking "Why" reveals nothing of his own feelings or attitudes. "Why" can only be asked when trust is high, that is, after you have received permission to ask.

In the inner conversations that we all have don't try to understand yourself by first asking "Why?" Instead try beginning with "What" and "How" you feel. "Why" is an invitation to intellectualizing which avoids feelings. The "Why" of your behavior will "float to the surface" indirectly if you focus on your feelings, not your explanations. For example, a frequent inner dialogue is: "Why am I overweight? I don't know. I just eat too much."

or

"I eat too much, because I'm depressed . . . have strong oral needs . . . don't know appetite from hunger . . . want to be self-destructive . . . want to insulate myself from men's/women's advances . . ." and on and on.

Any or many of these reasons might be accurate, but so what? Insight doesn't necessarily make for change. In fact, insight can make life worse. If, in this instance, weight doesn't go down, the insight can add deeper feelings of defeat.

A healthier internal dialogue would go this way:

"How do I feel about being overweight? I feel out of control and defeated. What does it feel like to be out of control? I feel foolish and angry for getting myself into this state. What am I going to do with my anger? Maybe I can turn the energy toward being thinner . . . and so on."

Overweight is a deeply complicated state of body and mind. The above dialogue is only a beginning to cope with this problem. But how about pausing to become more aware of how *you feel on writing down* how *you feel just before you overeat. You might then become more able to redirect the energy away from the eating.*

Notice this approach doesn't attempt to disown certain feelings, such as gorging. Instead the idea is to accept the feeling whatever it is, and redirect its energy. It is impossible to get rid of a specific feeling. To try to do so only increases internal conflict, because will power is pitted against the "disowned" feeling.

The question "Why" in inner dialogue is usually directed toward analyzing yourself and dissecting a particular behavior and its related feelings. The "How" and "What" questions, instead, help to get more acquainted with yourself. So if a person writes down or thinks through how *he feels when he has the impulse to, for example, gorge, he is gaining greater awareness of the feeling. There is the chance then to add on some other patterns of eating in addition to gorging. If this is done, the gorging will become less a primary way of eating and weight loss could naturally occur.*

This same approach to "Why" questions in the inner dialogue applies to other behavior. For example, the person who is unhappy with his or her homosexual drives won't get far asking:

"Why am I this way?"

or

"Why *am I attracted to him or her?*"

If instead the person gets more acquainted with his or her homosexual feelings by asking "What" *and* "How" *questions, the person might decide to* "add on" *some additional ways of relating sexually. This might mean adding on bisexuality or a shift over to heterosexuality, or becoming more accepting of the preference for the same sex.*

"Would you be upset if I asked you something?"

☐ It may be a sneak question, designed to tie your hands. It cannot be answered, because who knows what he is going to ask? For instance, if this twisty person asks, "How much money do you make?" or "Will you lend me $500?" or "Are you screwing your secretary?"—you *should* be upset. But if you answered "No," then the asker has you over a barrel.

☐ Sometimes this is a mousy question from an insecure person who can't stand even a hint of disapproval or rejection. For instance, he will say, "Would you be upset if . . ." If the answer is "No," then he proceeds to ask, "Do you like what I'm wearing?" He not only is afraid of rejection, he is desperately trying to make his feelings, his inquiries, his uncertainties important to the other person.

☐ The person who feels that a question may be too upsetting would do better to say, "There is something I want to ask you, but please let me know if it upsets you." This is better, but it is still not good. There's a patronizing nuance here that the other person really shouldn't be upset, but the questioner feels that he is the kind of unstable person who will be upset.

☐ In some instances a modification of this question is a sensitive way of asking permission to broach a specific topic. For example, "Would you be upset if I asked you about marriage?"

"Would you do me a favor?"

☐ This is manipulative talk that asks the other person to sign a blank check. He is being asked to say "yes" without knowing what he is saying "yes" to. This kind of talk lacks openness and does not put first things first. The honest way to communicate this message would be something like, "I've got to take the car to the garage this morning and I don't want to spend the whole day waiting for it. Would you be willing to follow me down there and drive me home and then drive me back when the car is ready?" This outlines the extent of the favor and allows the other person to agree to do it or explain why he doesn't want to or can't do it.

"Yes, but . . ."

☐ Underlying all meanings of this is the fact that it is not a message that can be taken literally. The "yes" is not really "yes." It is not agreement, but a way of interrupting. It's a trick because the "yes" implies agreement. Therefore there's no reason for the other person to say anything more. Behind this are various nuances such as:

□ A defense. It's a response to a busybody who wants to tell the yes-butter how to conduct his life. A more effective put-off would be to say something like, "Thank you, but your advice does not apply to my problem." Or, "You do not understand me or my problems."

□ A self-pity whine used by persons unable to make decisions or accept responsibilities. The other person can be suckered into spending his time, energy and imagination trying to help the speaker with his problem, but his every suggestion will be answered, "Yes, but I can't do that . . ." or "I tried that . . ." or "I'm not the type." This can drive a psychologically unsophisticated, good-hearted person crazy.

□ A sincere attempt to cope with impractical advice. A more effective way to handle this kind of advice would be to say, "I appreciate that you are trying to help me, but I'm not in the right state to listen to your suggestions at the moment."

Here is one way to deal with a "yes, but . . ." person: "I'm confused by what you just said. You said 'yes,' but what did you say 'yes' to?"

"You don't really want to know."

□ Testing. "Do you really care about what happened/what I think/what I'm going to do/what he said/how I feel?" Also a test of the degree of interest: "Do you *really* want to know or are you just feigning interest?"

☐ Condescending. "You don't really need to know. It wouldn't mean anything to you if I told you."

☐ Insulting. "It's none of your business."

If you seriously want to know and you think you have indicated your interest, then "You don't really want to know" is an insult. The other person is telling you what you want. How does he know what you want?

"You make me" messages

☐ In most instances the speaker is inappropriately blaming the other person for the way the speaker feels. If the speaker felt secure in himself, this would not happen. But the person who says "You make me" is admitting that he is not in control of his emotions; they are governed, at that moment, by the other person.

This kind of reaction is a crippler. The speaker has reduced his options of responding by admitting that he is not in charge of his life. See "You make me mad" (below) for explanation of how this crippling mechanism works, and some thoughts on how one can learn to be more aware of one's feelings in order to develop other ways of handling the situation.

☐ Most of these "You make me" messages radiate discomfort. "You make me mad." "You make me upset." "You make me happy." "You make me love you." All of these, even the ones about love and happiness give off the feeling of discomfort, because the speaker is "reacting" rather than "owning" his own feelings.

"You make me mad."

☐ Tom is talking down to Sam. Sam resents it and says, "You make me mad." The implication here is that Tom "pushes a button" and Sam reacts by getting mad. Tom "made" him get mad. Sam had no control over whether or not he got mad.

By saying this, Sam has admitted he is not in charge of his feelings. He is insecure. Instead of saying "You make me mad," it would be better if Sam were to ask himself, "What is it about Tom that makes me mad?" If the answer is "Because he's always talking down to me," then Sam is ready to do something about it. He has isolated the "mad-making" mechanism. Now he can be in charge. The next thing Sam should ask himself is: "What am I going to do about it?" This is important, because the more choices he has at his disposal, the better he will be able to handle his feelings toward Tom.

> What are some of Sam's choices?
> 1. He can walk away from Tom.
> 2. He can tell Tom how he feels . . . not by saying, "You make me mad," but by saying, "This manner you have of talking down to me, of partronizing me, is something I don't like. I wish you would stop it. If not, I don't want to talk anymore!"
> 3. He can give Tom a little more time and see what happens.
> 4. He can decide that it's unimportant and put up with Tom.
> 5. He can be hostile, but conceal his hostility behind humor.

In each individual case there are countless options. But the options cannot be exercised as long as the person thinks that the other one "made him mad."

☐ A very slightly different nuance is that Sam means "I'm really mad at you, but I don't want to take responsibility for how I feel so I'm blaming my feelings on you." If I were to say, "I am mad," you might say, "That's tough" or "I couldn't care less." So I protect myself by blaming my feelings on you. Rather than "protecting" yourself, why not either work out a better relationship or get more distance?

"You make me nervous."

☐ This is one of those "you" messages that nurtures helplessness. The underlying meaning is: "I am not in control of the situation. You have the power to make me feel nervous or anxious." This person may be very insecure and easily made to feel inadequate. Or he can be absolutely realistic. Jack, for instance, is drunk and driving seventy-five miles an hour. Max says, "You make me nervous. Let me drive." He means exactly what he says.

"You mustn't cry" or "Don't cry."

☐ Why not? Tears are appropriate if the person is in physical or emotional pain. Crying can be therapeutic.

☐ "Stop it. You're making me uncomfortable." The message, which is meant to be received as sympathetic and reassuring, is really not. The speaker has little or no empathy with the other. All he wants is for the other person to stop crying, because tears upset him. Many people are made extremely uncomfortable by tears (and other displays of emotion) because they are so out of touch with their own unshed tears (or unexpressed emotions).

☐ The speaker reveals that he doesn't understand the situation.

"WHY DON'T YOU" MESSAGES

☐ "Why don't you move to the suburbs?" John asks Tom. John, as the reader might guess, lives in the suburbs. Tom now has to explain why he does not want to move to the suburbs.

This kind of question puts the other person in a "one-down" inferior position. Unless the two are on excellent terms, he usually feels that his judgment has been challenged so that he has to justify himself. There is probably no real reason why Tom should explain to John why he does not want to move to the suburbs, but he does. And he resents it. He also resents John's having "forced" him to do it. See "You make me" messages.

☐ There is one circumstance when a "why don't you" is justified. If Tom had said to John, "I don't know what to do. We are going to have a baby and we've been looking at larger apartments. But the rents are more than I can swing."

Now Tom has, in effect, offered to make a "contract" with John. He has made it clear that he would like John's opinion on what he should do. Now John can suggest, "Why don't you move to the suburbs?" No challenge or criticism is involved in this case.

If Tom had not established such a "contract," but John felt strongly that Tom would be better off in the suburbs, the way to communicate this would be with an "I" message. He could say something like, "I was thinking just the other day how you might enjoy some of our friends in our suburb. Have you ever thought about moving out of the city?"

This is neither a criticism nor a put-down. John shows that he likes Tom, that he thinks Tom would fit in well with his friends and would enjoy having him for a neighbor. He obviously considers him a compatible person. With this "I" message Tom is not made to feel defensive the way he would be if John said bluntly, "Why don't you move to the suburbs?" He can say what he thinks about the suburbs without having to accept or challenge John's statement.

"You ought to stop smoking."

☐ This is a valid message if the speaker is the other person's physician. Then it is an honest communication based upon a doctor-patient relationship.

☐ If the speaker is not a physician, this is busybodying. A person's health is his private property. No one has the right to tell him what to do about it—unless requested to do so. In this case, one can label the speaker as self-righteous and less interested in the other person's health than in setting himself up as a model.

☐ If this is a sincere message from a person who really cares, a better way to put it would be, "You know, I'm really concerned about your smoking. It worries me."

"You're never on time."

☐ An exasperated attack. It seems to be straightforward but conceals the speaker's angry feelings. It would be better to be open about these feelings and say something like, "I get so angry with you because you are almost always late when we have a date. I think that means you don't care about me or my feelings and that hurts. So between being angry and being hurt, my relationship with you is not very pleasant these days. I wish I could work this out with you."

☐ The word "never" is code for strong feelings which would usually be better expressed directly and openly. For instance: "I'm really angry at you for being late so often."

V

Hidden Meanings Between Associates and Acquaintances

*B*etween business associates and acquaintances it is often not worth the energy to try to get the hidden meanings out in the open. But often there is value in keeping tuned into possible hidden meanings in what is being said. And, even more important, a better understanding may transform an acquaintance into a friend.

The following section includes many examples of talking down to the listener. It is important to be aware of how this is done. It can help you with that uneasy feeling you get when someone talks down to you. Achieving this objectivity is preferable to suffering the pervasive uneasiness that results from being put down and not understanding how it happened.

"Are you getting anything out of this?"

☐ It's possible to take this at face value. A teacher asking a child "Are you getting anything out of this?"

really wants to know. A businessman who has set up seminars for colleagues might ask "Are you getting anything . . ." and mean it as a sincere quest for information.

☐ At another level, the question may carry the hidden meaning: "I'm not getting anything out of this, but before I say so I want to have my judgment confirmed." This person tends to distrust his own feelings or judgment.

☐ At still another level, there's a hidden insult. "If you're getting anything out of this, you're even stupider than I thought you were." The tone of voice can be the tip-off here.

☐ A fourth possibility: "Stop goofing off and start paying attention." This is a suspicious reprimand, reflecting the speaker's suspicion that he is wasting his time on you.

"As you well know, . . ."

☐ The speaker betrays his need to be superior. He talks as if he were a teacher lecturing a student, although he may in fact be addressing a peer. This kind of person tends to overreact if his assumed superiority is challenged.

When you hear this kind of talk, one reaction is to pull away and give yourself distance. Another reaction is to become hostile or sarcastic. Maybe either one of these choices is not appropriate for you in the specific situation. So what to do?

One useful choice is to ask yourself: "Why does this person have such a need to talk in such a superior or arrogant manner?" You might decide that it is out of a feeling of inferiority. If he didn't feel inferior why would he want to put energy into acting superior and using phrases such as "As you well know"?

"As you may remember . . ."

☐ "I am superior to you and want to keep my distance, therefore I use this aloof and patronizing method of jogging your memory."

☐ "You clod! You should remember."

☐ This could be a legitimate lead-in depending on the context.

"Be back in a moment."

☐ "Moment" is used for all kinds of time spans ranging from thirty seconds to half an hour—even more. This often means that the speaker feels some guilt about leaving, so he says "moment" when it will be "minutes." The person who is expecting the speaker back in a "moment" is justified in becoming hurt or angry when he does not show up for a significant length of time. It would be better to say, "Be back in ten minutes." This exact estimate of time shows courtesy and consideration. On the other hand, "I'll be back in a moment" is an example of how guilty feelings can make a situation worse.

"Believe me."

☐ This is an attempt to become believable by asking to be accepted as honest. The person who prefaces a statement with "Believe me" is implying that at other times he lies. His very insistence that the listener believe him raises the suspicion that he may be lying at that very moment.

"Chick"

☐ Male chauvinist label for a woman. You can be pretty sure that the man needs to feel that women (or this woman) are not his equal. He is insecure and the label makes him feel more competent and more male—since a chick is the last word in helplessness.

☐ How would it go over if a woman called a man "pup"?

"Don't call me, I'll call you."

The question is: How do you deal with this rejection? For some people this message can trigger a depression. Depression is often caused by anger turned inward in the form of "What's wrong with me?" "Why can't I get the person to like me?"

Others don't get depressed by the rejection expressed in "Don't call me, I'll call you." Their need to be liked by a specific person is not that great. At a deeper level they accept and like themselves enough to prevent dependency on being liked by a specific person. People who are not so needy of friendship often end up with many friends, because the lack of need or dependency allows them to be more themselves. They are therefore more truly equipped to be friends.

"Don't get me wrong."

☐ This is defensive and a backward message. A more direct way of putting it would be, "I want you to understand me on this." By saying, "Don't get me wrong," the speaker is delivering a negative communication. "Don't" and "wrong" are down words. People on the defense have fewer ways of communicating than people who feel comfortable.

☐ This often means "I expect to be misunderstood (taken wrong)." And this person keeps getting in deeper and deeper just because he expects to. It's a self-fulfilling prophecy. If he expects to be taken wrong, he is probably acting in a way that will make people take him wrong.

"Don't take yourself so seriously."

☐ "I don't take you that seriously!"

Psychologizing is part of the hostility to this message. The speaker presumes to tell the other person how he feels about himself by saying he takes himself too seriously. To not psychologize would be to say, "I think you take yourself too seriously." This is an opinion and there might be room for discussion.

☐ "Don't take yourself so seriously" can be an effective put-down to indefensible arrogance.

"*Far be it from me to say . . .*"

☐ Oh, this is slippery talk. Watch out. Of course, he's going to say whatever it is. The person who employs this phrase frequently is someone who by nature says he is going to do one thing and then proceeds to do another. And usually under cover of imposing pomposity.

"*Frankly, . . .*"

☐ Why is the speaker saying this? Couldn't it very likely be that he/she isn't usually candid, and maybe there is good reason to doubt the person's truthfulness even though "frankly" is included in the sentence?

☐ "Frankly" might also imply that you are being let in on something, a special bit of information or deeper thought. But then "frankly" is patronizing! The speaker pats you on the head and labels his message with "frankly" in order that you will know that what you are hearing is special.

"*Game plan*" as in "*What's your game plan?*" or "*Here's the game plan.*"

☐ This is one of those "once-removed" phrases that shows the speaker wants to be impersonal, does not want to become significantly involved with the person he's talking to or the project under discussion. If he were more open, he would say, "What are you going to do?" or "Here's what I think we should do."

There's a hidden clue in this phrase, as in most "game" phrases, to the nature of the speaker. He is probably impersonal, and highly competitive. He operates on the idea that there has to be a winner and a loser in every relationship, encounter or episode— even in marriage. And he intends to be the winner. The idea of cooperation or mutuality is alien to the speaker. He tends to scorn them as signs of weakness.

"Have you ever considered doing . . ."

☐ Officious and down-putting. It implies that the other person is too stupid to have considered whatever the speaker is about to suggest. Could you hold the hand of the person to whom you were saying, "Have you ever considered taking your daughter to a psychologist . . . mowing your lawn . . . doing something about your hair?" A kinder phrasing, if the speaker feels he must intrude, is to say, "I'd really like to help you figure out some way of coping with your daughter's shoplifting . . . or planning your work so you'll have time for yourself, etc."

"How do you mean that?"

When you want to know more—particularly about the other person's feelings—this is often an effective invitation to say more. The word "how" is a much softer, more inviting word that "why" or "what." Compare these three messages:
    "How do you mean that?"

"What do you mean by that?"
"Why do you mean that?"

"I don't want you to think that I am picking on you . . . angry with you . . . dissatisfied with your work."

☐ Yes, he does. No one ever says, "I don't want you to think that I love you . . . that you are doing a marvelous job, etc." This statement means exactly what the speaker says it doesn't. He's a patronizing fellow who doesn't think the other person is strong enough to accept criticism, so he veils it in ambiguities, patting himself on the back for his "tact." He also considers himself the superior of the other person.

"I do the best I can."

☐ "Get off my back." "Quit picking on me." The person who says this is often a whiner.

☐ In some cases, it means exactly what it says, with the additional sense of "And if you don't like it, that's tough."

"I know it's none of my business but . . ."

☐ The speaker wants to butt into the other person's business and does so by acknowledging that he is butt-ing in. This is usually intrusive and not helpful.

☐ It can be a gentle way of intruding and being helpful. The situation usually determines the real meaning. If his advice takes the listener's problem and feelings into account, there is a genuine desire to help. If he simply wants to show how much better *he* could manage his life, get rid of him as soon as possible.

☐ "I know what is best for you, so whether you ask me or not I'm going to tell you."

There are many messages that bring two people close and others that add distance. This one usually adds distance. It is presumptuous. You haven't asked him—and it doesn't help to have the preface "I know it's none of my business, but. . . ."

"I'll tell you later."

☐ This is a sliding-out-from-under phrase. The speaker does not want to tell whatever it is. His vague promise to tell later is not just a postponement, it's a way of saying "no" without having to say the actual word. People who use this and other vague negatives are unwilling to risk the rejection and anger that they think a "no" will trigger.

You don't have to accept this put-off. You deserve a more specific message that tells you when. Why not respond with something like this: "I feel up in the air having it left this way. How about telling me when you will let me know."

"I'll try harder."

☐ "Shut up and get off my back." When the speaker is in an inferior position (a child to parent, an employee to employer), he is ostensibly promising future behavior to a superior, but he might not mean to keep his promise. All he wants is for the other to stop harping on the subject. The promise is his only weapon, his only way to get the superior to stop criticizing him while he still acts in a seemingly contrite and obedient manner.

☐ Between equals it probably means just what it says.

"I'm not kidding."

☐ This is a threat. The speaker is angry and emphasizes his words with this ominous phrase. He means business. Be warned.

☐ "You are making a mistake by not listening to what I say. And that mistake may hurt you."

☐ "Take me seriously"—a plea.

"I'm not sure." "I'm not sure right now."

☐ This is usually one of those "no's" where the speaker is afraid to say "no." He fears rejection, anger, and argument; sometimes he just doesn't dare express his feelings about anything. This kind of answer is indefinite; it doesn't deal with the question.

And if he is not sure now, when will he be sure? Never.

□ This can mean exactly what it says: "I'm not sure or I'm not sure right now." But when this is said it often leaves the other person waiting or hanging on "When will you be sure?" Therefore give some idea of when you will be sure. For example, "I'm not sure now but I'm going to think about this and I want to talk with you more tomorrow."

"I'm so busy I just don't have a minute for myself."

□ Anne has three preschool children, no help, and her husband works days and goes to law school at night. She means exactly what she says.

□ This could reflect a person who is desperately seeking approval and acceptance. John never turns down a request for his services. It is important for him to feel needed. He feels that if he turns down a request to work on a project, a committee, a campaign, people will see how unworthy he is. He is hooked on the approval he gets for working so hard. And on another level, he fears that if he doesn't keep busy, everything will fall apart—especially him.

□ "Feel sorry for me."

□ It can mean bewilderment and disorganization. This person just never has had his life in order. He doesn't know how to manage his life to make room for himself. He's at the mercy of his own insecurities and weaknesses. He keeps himself busy with makeshift activities, because he is scared of doing nothing. Then he would be alone.

"I'm sure someone as intelligent as you are . . ."

☐ He wants something. He may simply want to make the other feel appreciated, but it's more likely that he's trying to put the other in a position where he feels he must do what the speaker requests or think as the speaker thinks to earn his regard or retain his esteem.

☐ It is a tip-off to arrogance. The speaker feels entitled to make judgments on others' intelligence.

"I'm uptight right now."

☐ An absolutely straightforward way of describing a situation in which the speaker is emotionally stretched to the utmost. It is worthy discussing since it is a relatively new bit of jargon. A simple exercise can "manufacture" uptightness right now. Press the palms of your hands hard against each other, hard enough so that a tremor develops. This is literally being uptight. It is similar to the kind of pressure that develops when a person has taken on too much work, tries to squeeze in one more errand before train or plane time, etc.

Uptightness is also caused by ambivalence, being pulled in many directions at once. It is the diametrically opposite pressure of that experienced by the palm-pushing exercise described above, but it is equally energy draining.

The opposite of uptight is to have all one's energy moving in one direction, without conflict, hence, a sense of flowing.

☐ The use of "right now" gives this message an added dimension of clarity. The speaker is not uptight all the time. He recognizes that. He is simply letting his audience know that right now there is more pressure on him than he can cope with easily.

"In my humble opinion . . ."

☐ False humility. He is really saying that he is so much more intelligent and well informed than his audience that he has to soften his views by pretending to be modest. Otherwise the other person will be crushed. It's possible to call such a person's bluff, but it usually isn't worth it. To confront him and suggest he express himself straightforwardly implies that one has a stake in the relationship. It is usually difficult to invest much in a relationship with this kind of person. By putting himself down, the speaker confuses the communication—usually hopelessly.

"In my judgment . . ."

☐ This is politician's talk. "In my judgment, the dollar

will be devalued . . . taxes will be increased . . . prices will go down." People who take themselves very seriously talk about their judgment as if it were something separate from themselves, a kind of appendix.

A better way to phrase such pronouncements is "I believe" or "I think prices will go down." Using the word "judgment" separates the speaker from his feelings and thoughts.

"I owe it all to my wife/husband/ mother/boss/teacher/etc."

☐ Not true. Who does the speaker think will believe him? The tip-off to the phoniness of this statement is the word "all." There would be more integrity evidenced if he said, "I owe a tremendous amount to my wife/etc."

☐ False modesty. It doesn't work and it is so transparent that one wonders why the speaker uses it. Take an absurd example like, "I owe everything to the hundred thousand dollars that I won in the lottery." This is inaccurate. He had to have had the initiative to buy the ticket and organized enough not to lose the stub.

"It depends."

☐ This is often a way of saying "no" without having to face the consequences directly.

If the person completes the message with, for instance, "It depends on information that I won't have until tomorrow," then it's not a cop-out.

"It doesn't really matter."

☐ "I don't really matter." The deceptive pronoun "it" really means "I." This is the case in such statements as "It makes me angry." (Translation: "I make myself angry.") "It's late." (Translation: "I'm late.")

☐ "Feel sorry for me." This person is saying, "So many things have gone wrong . . . go wrong . . . will go wrong for me that this one doesn't really matter." And there's often a deeper meaning of "Feel sorry for me and you damn well better feel guilty, too." If he knows that you feel guilty, that adds to his childish satisfaction.

"I told you so."

☐ Beyond the obvious sanctimonious implications of this, there's an interior meaning of "You didn't follow my advice. Now it's your problem." The speaker washes his hands of all responsibility.

"It makes me nervous."

☐ The real meaning is "*I* make myself nervous." But if the speaker puts it that way, then he is faced with having to do something about his nervousness. If he keeps it at a distance with "it," then it becomes easier to blame the nervousness on something "out there," a particular person, flying in an airplane, or whatever. The speaker would be more helpful to himself if he were to say, "I get nervous when I talk with John." Once he has said this, he can decide whether talking with John is rewarding enough or necessary enough to put up with the anxiety involved—or whether he really has to fly or perhaps should seek an alternate mode of transportation, etc.

If the speaker thinks in terms of "I make myself nervous when I talk with John . . . when I fly in an airplane," he has a better chance of working through the nervousness and hence coping better with John or flying in airplanes.

"I won't take no for an answer."

☐ The speaker is indicating that he suspects he is going to *have* to take "no" for an answer, but he wants more than just the word "no." He wants some explanation. Why did you decide to say "no"?

☐ A second level of meaning is: "I want to be closer to you, to know how you think and what your standards and values are. I want to know what is behind your decision, not just to hear the 'no' that represents the top of the iceberg of your thoughts and feelings."

"Just a minute."

☐ This is a simple stalling device—sometimes stalling for time, at other times cutting off a person's conversation or actions in order to impose one's own will.

☐ "I want your attention for a period of time . . . probably not just *one* minute. I want to interrupt whatever you are saying or doing in order to make my opinions heard."

"Labeling"

The use of labels like "Chick" usually indicate that the speaker is insecure with people. He cannot or will not look behind the label to see the person. Using labels is a way of keeping threatening ideas and feelings at a distance. The speaker will never have to analyze his feelings about blacks if he labels them as "niggers." He will never have to face the fact that women make him uneasy if he can label strong women as "women's libbers" or "ball breakers." The labeler is usually rigid, intolerant, fearful, insecure (to use some labels of my own!).

"Let's . . ."

☐ "Let's" is a dangerous, manipulative word— dangerous because it masquerades as an open, sharing word. It's used to soften up the other person. "Let's should be understood as "I" as in "Let's buy a new rug." (Translation: "I'd like to buy a new rug.") "Let's go out to eat." (Translation: "I don't feel like cooking"—or possibly, "I'd like a good meal for a change.")

"Let's face it."

☐ The speaker insists that the listener agree with him and see the situation the way he sees it. He will brook no divergence of opinion. Often this statement is an introduction to a proposal that measures be taken to remedy the situation—measures that usually will hurt someone else: emotionally, financially, socially. "Let's face it. John doesn't belong in this club." "Let's face it. Joan is impossibly inaccurate. We can't have a woman like that in the office." "Let's face it, the country is going to the dogs. I'm not going to support either party this year."

"Let me make this perfectly clear . . ."

☐ The speaker is really saying: "I'll tell you what I want you to know and how you should think about it." The implication that he knows how clear or how muddy his listener's perceptions are at any moment is a dead giveaway to the superficiality of this communication. It assumes a skill that no one possesses. The phrase is a clue to arrogance and insecurity, two states that often go hand in hand.

"Let me think about it."

☐ Occasionally the speaker really means what he says. He's not sure. He wants to think. His instinct is to say "no," but he really wants to explore his feeling on the subject.

☐ The answer is "no," but he doesn't want to come out with "no." This is a particularly devious kind of turn-down, because the speaker is asking the permission of the other person for time to think about whatever it is. And all the time, his mind is made up. It's just one more way of saying "no" without saying "no."

"Look on the bright side of things."

☐ A turn-off. This "helpful" hint is just cheap, superficial advice. All it conveys is a lack of understanding for the other person.

☐ Decoded, this may mean: "I don't want to hear any more."

☐ The speaker is out of touch with his own feelings. He mistakenly thinks feelings can be switched off and on at command, because he has never dared let himself feel. Thus it is impossible for him to empathize with someone else's feelings. A person who is in trouble cannot appropriately switch off his distress and escape into enumerating the good things in his life. He must deal with his problems first.

"Nobody told me."

☐ "I'm feeling sorry for myself."

☐ "You should have told me." There is a secondary meaning here of "I don't dare say what I feel, which is

that you should have told me what was going on, so I
just complain weakly that 'nobody told me.' "

"Nothing is wrong."

☐ "Something is wrong, but I don't want to talk about
it."

☐ "Nothing" may mean "everything." At times this
may be a reaching out for help, a way of provoking
further questions by pretending to be self-contained.
It can mean "Keep on asking what's wrong until I get
up my courage to talk to you about my problems."

"Oh, it was nothing."

☐ This is "martyr talk." It can be translated as "I am
nothing." This response is used by people who get so
uncomfortable when praised that they have to make a
disclaimer. They cannot bring themselves to say,
"Thank you. I felt good about it, too." Perfectionists
also use this kind of phrase, because they find it hard
to accept praise. They can never live up to their own
perfectionist standards. Perfectionists are also
martyrs—rather special hair-shirted martyrs.

"One would think . . ."

☐ This prefaces such messages as: "One would think
he would do it differently." "One would think he
wouldn't put up with that." "One would think that he

would not be so extravagant now that. . . ." This way of talking is close to the ultimate in impersonality. The speaker does not want to take responsibility for what he is saying. By using "One would think" the implication is that the thought just floated in the window or happened to appear magically.

☐ This expression is used by people who like to make adverse judgments about others, but are not willing to come out and say, "I think his ideas are foolish" or "I think he made a stupid decision."

"Really."

☐ This is a challenge (and often a rather supercilious one). John says, "I think the gas turbine engine is the only possible engine of the future." Jasper replies, "Really?" Jasper may mean to suggest that only a simpleminded person would hold such a view. On the other hand, he may be impressed. You'll know by his intonation.

☐ It could indicate amazement. John says, "I think the gas turbine engine is the only possible engine of the future." Joan replies, "Really!" She's amazed at John's grasp of science and technology.

☐ A put-down. John says, "I think etc." Dr. Jason Jones, the famed engineer, replies, "Really." He is saying, "My dear fellow, that is such a simplistic, superficial statement that I'm not going to dignify it with a thoughtful response."

☐ A defense. While the word may be used in some cases as a legitimate way to underscore an opinion ("It's really great." "She's really talented."), it often carries the nuance of "This time I'm telling the truth." There's an implication that the speaker must give a signal when he has decided to tell the truth, because his usual mode is to shade or distort.

"Speaking frankly . . . to be perfectly frank . . . to tell the truth . . . to be completely honest . . ."

☐ Watch out. These are all danger signs. The speaker is a slippery character.

☐ Flattery. Trying to flatter the listener by implying that the speaker is usually less than honest, but with the listener he is going to be honest. The message: "You should feel privileged, because I am going to do something that is out of character for me. I am going to be honest." Perhaps he will be, but don't count on it.

☐ Deceitful insult. The speaker thinks so little of the listener that he believes the simple fact of stating his honesty is enough to convince. Examine with skepticism all statements that follow these phrases.

"Take it easy."

☐ A goodwill gesture, similar to "Be well."

□ What is "it"? Does the speaker mean "Take yourself easily"? Why should he say that? You are important to yourself. You *should* take yourself seriously. But if the speaker is truly concerned, a better way of conveying the message might be: "You are overreacting to the situation—at least the way I see it. I think you will be better off if you try to be less emotional about this."

□ Does he mean "Relax and don't be so hard on yourself?" In this case, he could say, "I'm worried about you. You're working too hard. Can't you slow down a little so that things will be a little easier for you?"

"That's interesting."

The ear has to be tuned to this one. Just how much charge does the word "interesting" carry?

□ "You're boring me, but I don't want to come out and say so."

□ "There's a pause in your flow of words. I'd better say something. Something polite and meaningless."
   Occasionally this means that the listener finds the other's conversation or information truly interesting. In that case, he is more likely to say, "That's very interesting," in order to convey conviction. Since "very" is such a hollow word, it would be much better to say, "I never thought of that before . . . never heard of that before . . . tell me more."

"That's your problem."

☐ There's almost always hostility here. Whether it is said in an intimate or family or work situation, the true meaning is, "I'm not involved and I don't want to be involved and I *won't* be involved. Don't count on me for help."

☐ Another equally hostile meaning is, "That's tough. You got yourself into it, now get yourself out."

☐ On certain occasions, this can be a supportive, constructive message. It has taken on a special meaning in group therapy sessions where it's used to indicate that a person should take more responsibility for managing his own life. Here it means "Go ahead. You can cope with that problem."

"To say the obvious . . ."

☐ A person who uses this phrase should be aware that it is saying something about him, something unpleasant.

☐ The speaker is giving himself permission to be boring. It is often used by nonstop talkers as an excuse for hogging the air time.

☐ It can be a way for the speaker to prevent others from suggesting he is boring.

☐ The phrase may be completely phony. The speaker wants to sound important, cool, urbane, but he is insecure and does not think that he is any of these.

□ It is condescending. He wants to make the point that what he is going to say is commonplace to him, but definitely not to his less-informed listener.

"Very"

□ Often this is an indication of being ill-at-ease, unsure of oneself. The person who sprinkles her/his speech with "very's" is probably insecure. "I had a very nice time." "That's a very pretty dress." "It's a very interesting book." These statements show that the person feels he or she has to underscore his or her feelings if they are to be accepted or taken seriously. "Very" is such an over-used word that the speaker, rather than underscoring, dilutes the power and clarity of his message.

"We'll see."

□ Often used as a put-off by a person in power. For example, an employee asks for a raise and the boss says "We'll see." This shuts off the communication and probably also conveys "Don't bring it up again. I'll tell you when you'll get a raise; don't ask."

The employee should not let the matter rest there unless he really does not want that raise. A "We'll see" response is best countered by a question like "Well, this means a lot to me. When can we talk about it again?" Or possibly—and here you have to be sure of the person you're talking to—"Well,

I'd certainly like to see it in my next paycheck. When do you think you'll be able to let me know on this?" The employee should not worry about incurring the ill will of his boss by these further questions. If the boss does not want to (or is unable to) give him the raise, he already feels bad and the questions won't make him feel any worse. If it was an honest "We'll see," then he won't mind spelling out the facts—that he has to wait until after the monthly meeting or whatever.

"We must get together."

□ A left-handed social amenity that means "I really don't want to tie myself down to see you at a specific time, but I don't want you to know that." The speaker is sending out a message that he wants the other to accept as a "caring" message, although he doesn't really care.

How does one respond to this? "Yes, we must?" But then what? In a way, it's like the socially accepted response to the inquiry "How are you?" "Fine."

□ The word "must" is significant. Who says we "must" get together? A more direct communication is to say, "I'd like to get together with you." This elicits a reply like, "So would I. How about Friday?" Or, if the other is not interested he can make another meaningless social noise and say something like, "Yes, we certainly should get together one of these days," which means "I'd rather not."

"We should see more of each other."

☐ Watch that Deceptive Pronoun. Does the "I" within the "We" represent one percent or 50 percent or 99 percent of the "we"? The effect of the "we" is to make the other person uncertain whether or not the speaker really does want to see more of him.

☐ The use of "should" injects a sense of guilt and duty. "I feel guilty that I don't see you more often. I know I should, but I don't really enjoy it."

"We should see more of each other. Give me a call."

☐ The addition of "Give me a call" reinforces the attempt at avoidance that occurs in the previous entry. The speaker is leaving it up to the other to initiate their next get-together, at the same time giving him the impression that he doesn't really care if he sees him again or not.

☐ With an obvious sincere person this might be taken literally. It would be better if it were stated more clearly because of the possibilities of misinterpretation. One way of putting it would be: "I had a great time and I'd like to see you again. I know you're busy, so give me a call when you have time."

*"We should see more of each other.
I'll call you one of these days."*

☐ This could be sincere but the odds are against it.

☐ An evasion. The speaker is saying, "Well, our meeting could have been worse and I know it means something to you, so I suppose I should indicate interest in getting together again, although I have no intention of it. And please don't try to get in touch with me."

"What do you mean?"

☐ A useful, efficient way of finding out more about what the speaker is talking about. But it is often more useful to substitute "How" for "What." "How" is a softer way of exploring meanings and feelings. Just take this example:

"I can't understand my husband." "What do you mean?" "I mean that I just don't understand him."

Now, substitute "how," and the exchange might go this way:

"I just can't understand my husband." "How do you mean that?" "Well, he's just so unpredictable. I don't know what to expect next."

*"Why aren't you married—a nice girl
like you?"*

☐ This one is loaded with messages. First and foremost, the speaker implies that the only way to live is to be married.

☐ What does "a nice girl like you" mean? It's patronizing. Can only "nice" people be married? And what about the word "girl"? Patronizing again. Marriage is something for women, not girls.

☐ This is often asked by a man as a way of getting to know a woman, particularly to get to know a lot about her personal life. It's an aggressive probe—an intrusion into the woman's personal feelings.

"You get on my nerves."

☐ This is a hostile message. See "You make me nervous" for an analysis of a similar message. The word "make" in that message implies that the other person has the power to force the speaker to be nervous. The speaker is admitting he reacts, not initiates. But in this case, the use of the word "get" means that the speaker is in charge. His nerves are not at the mercy of the other person. Instead, he is saying, in a rather threatening way, "You better back off. You are getting me nervous and I don't like it."

"You have to be patient . . . see both sides . . . bend a little, etc."

☐ A waste of breath. Who's going to listen seriously to a person expounding on what one "has to" do?

☐ Patronizing, insulting, meddling. The speaker has no right to tell anyone he "has to" do anything.

*It would be better to turn these into "I" messages and share
the feelings that lie behind the words. For instance: "I can
imagine you're angry about that. I would be. But I do wonder just what was in that person's mind when he acted that
way." This is forthright, does not deny the anger that is
present, but still leaves the door open to exploring what was
behind the words or action. It does not sermonize or set the
speaker up as holier than thou.*

"You must come over and see us."

☐ Most likely this is another of those social noises. It's
hard to differentiate between a sincere invitation,
which this might be, and a social noise. If the speaker
really means what he says, why not phrase it as a
direct invitation. "How about coming over Wednes-
day night? We'd really like to see you." This is understood as an invitation, but "You must come over, etc."
will not be heard as a real invitation by most people.
And the truth is, it probably isn't.

☐ It's a test of sorts. The speaker is timid and does not
quite dare invite the other over for fear his invitation
might be declined. So he says, "You must come
over . . ." to check out the response. If the other says,
"Oh, we'd love to," then he can go on and deliver an
invitation setting a time. If the response, "We'd love
to," does not elicit an invitation, then "You must come
over . . ." must be accepted as a meaningless social
noise. Well, not quite meaningless—it indicates a certain measure of goodwill.

"You never know about those things."

☐ This sanctimonious observation assumes that the listener "knows" what the speaker "knows" about a given situation. It covers his feelings of inadequacy. The speaker is not self-confident enough to say, "I'm really puzzled by this kind of thing," or "I don't know what to expect next." This would be an admission of defeat—one he doesn't dare make. People who use this phrase are usually insecure and "lost," no matter how self-possessed they may appear on the surface.

"You're driving me crazy."

This is tops in "you make me" language. The word "drive" means exactly that. The speaker is saying, "I am so out of control of my state of mind that you are not only making me crazy, but you are driving me to craziness. It's as if you were at the wheel of myself."

"You're resisting."

☐ "You're not behaving (or responding) the way I want you to." This is used by therapists and teachers to stifle disagreement, as in the following situation.

The patient says to his therapist, "I want to stop coming here, I don't think I'm getting anywhere." After some preamble, the therapist replies, "You're resisting." This asserts the therapist's superiority and gets the patient off the subject he initiated and forces him to defend himself. The therapist is once again in command.

"You weren't listening to me."

☐ This carries an unsuspectedly high emotional charge, heightened because the speaker does not know whether or not the other *was* listening. Because of this, there is no satisfactory answer. If the other responds, "I was listening," the speaker still feels angry. In addition, he feels shut off, because he's really asking for some feedback, some reassurance. A better way to express his distress would be: "I don't feel that I'm getting across to you. What is your reaction to what I've just said?"

VI

How to Guard Against the Deceptive Pronouns

*P*eople not only hide their meanings, they often hide themselves behind a pronoun. Even "I," that honest little pronoun, can be deceitful, hiding behind a "we" or "they." Even behind a "you." And then, there are times when "I" is used as a front man for a "you" message. It is necessary to learn how to detect these deceptions if one is to delve into the hidden meanings of person-to-person communications.

The phony "I" message is probably the easiest to detect. For instance, watch out for such "I" messages as "I think you are really much too defensive." Or this one: "I feel that you are making a mistake."

These are fakes. How can you tell? Easy. Does the statement reflect or reveal the speaker's feelings? If it does, then it is an honest, straightforward "I" message. If it does not, then it is a fake, an aggressive "you" message in drag.

Let's take the first statement: "I think you are really much too defensive." This reveals nothing whatsoever about how the speaker feels. Instead, he is telling the listener how the listener feels—"much too defensive." In the second statement, the same thing holds true. The speaker is really saying, "You are making a mistake." There is nothing about "I" in these two statements. However, if the speaker had said, "I'm very worried. I think you're making a mistake by not taking a vacation," that is something else. Now we know how the speaker feels. He has opened up his feelings of concern and explained why he thinks the other is making a mistake.

"We" is really "I's" twin brother in many situations—and probably the most consistently deceptive of all pronouns, because it is impossible to know who is "we" and how much weight each member of the "we" carries.

Let me explain what I mean by this. Take a classic "we" message: "We're so happy we never have any arguments, etc." The question arises, "Who is we?" Is it John? Is it Joan? Is it John and Joan? In this particular case, the "we" is almost always a sneaky "I," an "I" that may really be saying something like, "I wish I was sure that the reason we never have any fights is because we care so much for each other. I am afraid that the reason we never have any fights is that we don't dare to. Our relationship offers each of us a haven, a place to hide our inadequacies, and we don't want to rock the boat." Or it could mean, "I'm afraid the reason we don't have any fights is that John cares so little for me that he can't be bothered to fight, even when I do something that annoys him."

When the listener hears a "we," it is important to try to figure out "who is we?" Fifty percent Joan and fifty percent John? Or ten percent John and ninety percent Joan. Or is it one hundred percent Joan? No one, of course, can determine the exact percentages, and they will fluctuate from moment to moment, but it is important to get a sense of who carries the most weight in a particular "we" message.

Take the case of Mr. Summit, the big boss who is in charge of all the hiring and firing. He calls in Sam Sack and says, "Sam, I'm sorry, but we have decided we have to cut down the sales force. You'll find your check and severance pay at the cashier's cage."

Who is this "we" who decided to cut down the sales force. It has to be Mr. Summit. The next question is, "Why did Mr. Summit feel he had to hide behind we?" This is the important question for Sam Sack. It is very likely that the boss is truly a very insecure person who hates unpleasantness of any kind and personal confrontations in particular, so he uses "we" as a disguise for "I."

If Sam thinks this is the case, then he should go ahead and demand to know why he of all people is the one to be fired. He should point out that Joe Jock has not made as many sales as he has and that he has been on the staff longer than George Gladhand. There is a good chance that Mr. Summit will back down in face of this angry confrontation and keep Sam Sack on. Sam should understand that what he has done is not gain job security, but he has gained time to look around and find another position for himself. And after all, who wants to work for a boss who is so easily manipulated?

Then there is the possibility that the "we" was an honest "we" and Mr. Summit has given away something that he was supposed to keep quiet about. He may no longer be an autonomous "I." He may have taken on a silent partner, or the firm may have been absorbed by a larger firm in which he is no longer boss, just another executive.

How is Sam Sack to know which is the case? Well, he can't be certain, but he is entitled to ask a few leading questions, such as "Why?" I thought business was pretty good lately. Why do you have to cut down the sales staff?"

The boss may level with him at this point and tell him that the firm is under new ownership. This gives Sam Sack an opening to say something like, "Well, I understand. But this puts me in a very bad spot. I don't have enough to live on while I'm looking for a new job? How about keeping me on until I find a new job?"

This appeal might work because Mr. Summit may be so eager to preserve face in front of Sam and at the same time to reassure himself that he still counts for something around there that he will agree.

It might also happen that the boss would say, "Look, Sam, you're no damned good. You're the worst salesman on the force. You've got to go." This is hard to take, but at least it's an honest communication and Sam now knows where he stands. He also, if he is smart, has learned that it is time to take a look at his life-style and life goals. He may not be cut out to be a salesman. What would he rather do? Getting fired might be the best thing that ever happened to him. But he'll never know it unless he is able to analyze the "we" message and get more input from his boss.

"We" also offers a camouflage for dishonesty. When fourteen-year-old Flora Flirt tells her mother, "I stayed after school today because Nancy Nice and Sally Solid and I were working on the decorations for the Halloween Hop and then we went to The Chocolate Glop for a snack," mother is delighted that Flora has started going around with a desirable group of girls. What she doesn't realize is that Flora *did* work on the decorations with Nancy and Sally, but that the "we" who went to The Chocolate Glop was Sally and Frank Fumbler, an older teen-ager whom Flora's mother disapproves of.

In the same way, Allan Rover may call his wife and say, "I'm going to have to work late tonight with the rest of the guys to make up the annual sales report. So don't wait dinner. We'll go out and grab a bite." And he does. But the "we" who grab the bite is Allan and his secretary, not Allan and the guys.

"They" is another common disguise for "I." And let us also lump "everybody" in with this sneaky pronoun. Both of them usually turn out to be "I." Although occasionally "everybody" means "nobody," as any mother who has lived through the following scene can testify.

"Everybody is going to Jim's party," says Flora Flirt. "Why can't I go? They're not too old a crowd for me. Everybody in my class is going."

"Who?" asks her mother. "Who in your class is going?"

"Everybody!" shrieks Flora.

"All right, tell me just one girl and I'll call her mother and talk it over with her. If a lot of girls are going, perhaps it would be all right, although I don't like you going around with those older kids."

And, of course, it turns out that Flora can't come up with a single name of a girl in her class who's going to the party.

But back to "they." "They're all wearing short skirts again," a woman tells her husband. The hus-

band has just raised an eyebrow and suggested his
wife's hemline is a bit too high. "Who is they," he asks.
"Everybody," she answers. The fact is that she prides
herself on being a fashion setter and the first in her
crowd to wear a new style. Her "they" is really an "I."

The woman who says, "They made me go off my
diet. They absolutely insisted I have some dessert. I
couldn't refuse," is really saying, "I wanted that dessert so much I went off my diet."

And so it goes. "They" are not always Tom, Dick
and Harry, but often just an "I" that wants its own
sneaky way.

Some readers may be interested in going back
through the entries in this book and analyzing them
afresh in view of what they have learned about deceptive pronouns. In many cases, you will find that you
see even more hidden meanings in a given statement
than you did in the beginning. All it takes is practice,
once you understand how we use these little pronouns to hide behind. They really don't offer much
shelter against the person who knows how to listen.
And the man or woman who is striving for honest and
clear communication will work to clean out the deceptive pronounal underbrush from his conversation. It
is well worth the effort.

VII

Uncovering Hidden Meanings

A necessary question at the close of this book is how to talk with a person when you sense some hidden meaning to what is being said, and you care enough about the relationship to want to talk it through and into the open. You don't want the hidden meanings left unsaid. This is a delicate opportunity and there are guidelines to follow.

It won't work to confront when you want to get the hidden meaning out in the open. For example, "Why don't you say what you really mean? Quit playing games with me!" You may feel impatient and want to be this abrupt, but it won't succeed at getting into hidden meanings. Instead the confrontation will close the person down rather than invite him into opening up.

Another way that won't work is psychologizing. For example: "Don't you think what you really mean is that you have a need to be competitive with me." Even if this bit of psychologizing were exactly accurate, it won't help at talking more openly. It instead causes the same reaction as the confrontation, because telling another person what he is feeling (psychologizing) is a form of confrontation.

What will work is talking with your friend or loved one in a way that fosters trust and safety. This means inviting him to talk along with you as if you were walking along beside him, not pushing against him as in confronting or psychologizing.

Here is how this might go.

"I don't think I really matter to you."

"How do you mean?"

or,

"I have a lot I want to say, but first tell me more of what you are saying."

"Well, I just feel like I'm often taken for granted. You don't seem as affectionate for one thing."

"I don't think I have been as affectionate lately, but it is not because of you. You matter maybe even more to me now, even though I'm not showing it. I'm going through a lot in my work, and I guess it is showing in how I am with you."

"Sorry to hear about the work, but it is a relief to hear it isn't me. What is happening in the work?"

I hope this interchange conveys the sense of walking along beside each other, both being equal, neither one talking down or up to the other person. This quality of talk is what enabled one person to share feelings about affection and the other person to bring up feelings about work. This conversation instead could have gone this way:

"I don't think I really matter to you."

"Now why are you saying that? I'm doing the best I can."

"Well, I just feel taken for granted."

"I think you are insatiable. There is never enough."

"See, this is proof of what I just said. I don't really matter to you. If I did you wouldn't talk this way to me."

In this encounter they never got beyond the first layer of words. The meanings below the surface concerning affection and work never got to the surface. Probably the estrangement became deeper. If talk like this happens often enough the love relationship deteriorates. It becomes more comfortable to be distant and closed off. Then it often is just a matter of time before the relationship ends (even if the marriage goes on). Hidden meanings remain hidden. Misunderstandings become more embedded.

Relationships are eroded not by what is said. *Whatever* the message is, if it is gotten out there is the chance to talk it through and the relationship profits. Relationships are eroded by hidden meanings—the feelings and thoughts that are left unsaid.

Further Reading on Communication

Bach, George, and Peter Wyden, *Intimate Enemy: How to Fight Fair in Love and Marriage.* New York: Morrow, 1969. (Paperback: Avon)
A manual for fighting fairly between equal partners.

Dodson, Fitzhugh, *How to Parent.* Freeport, N.Y.: Nash, 1973. (Paperback: NAL)
A complete guide for both the emotional and intellectual development of the child from birth to six plus a section on discipline for school age children.

Gardner, Richard A., Dr. *Gardner's Stories About the Real World.* New York: Avon, 1976. (Paperback)
Rather than advice or admonition to children, this collection of stories to read to children can often be a preferable alternative.

Ginott, Haim, *Between Parent and Child.* New York: Avon, 1973. (Paperback)
Particularly useful for parents in adding to their skill to empathetically tune-in to the "coded" language a child is speaking through his or her behavior as well as the words.

Gordon, Thomas, *Parent Effectiveness Training.* New York: Wyden, 1975. (Paperback: NAL)
Completely describes a method of communicating with children that is superior to either permissiveness or authoritarianism.

Leshan, Eda, *What Makes Me Feel This Way?* New York: Macmillan, 1974. (Paperback)
A book to be read by children; could be catalyst for important discussion with parents.

Mornell, Pierre, *The Lovebook.* New York: Harper and Row, 1974.
A practical book on keeping a relationship close and at the same time free for growth as individuals.

Satir, Virginia, *Peoplemaking*. Palo Alto, CA: Science and Behavior, 1975. (Paperback: Science and Behavior)
An extraordinary book on human relations.

Satir, Virginia, *Making Contact*. Millbrae, CA: Celestial Arts, 1976.
Innovative techniques for learning the essence of making contact.

Satir, Virginia, *Self Esteem*. Millbrae, CA: Celestial Arts, 1976.
A simple and profound declaration of self-worth in the form of a poem.

Smith, Gerald Walker, *Couple Therapy*. New York: Collier, 1973. (Paperback)
Communication experiences for couples to enter into together followed by commentaries about marital interaction.

Suid, Murray, *Marriage, etc.* Reading, Mass.: Addison-Wesley, 1976.
An innovative and effective format for covering a wide range of personal issues concerning marriage.

About the Author

Dr. Gerald Smith is a psychologist in Belmont, California. He has done human relations work in the U.S. Air Force, Bechtel Corporation, Napa State Mental Hospital, San Quentin State Prison, Marriage Council of Philadelphia, Institute for Alcohol and Narcotic Addiction, Consultation Services of San Mateo County Mental Health Services, Mental Research Institute, and KPIX-TV.

His education includes an A.B. and M.B.A. from Stanford University, M.Div. from Pacific School of Religion, and Ed.D. from University of Pennsylvania. He is a member of the American Psychological Association and the Association for Humanistic Psychology.

An earlier book, *Couple Therapy,* is a series of communication experiences for couples to enter into together.

BOOKS OF RELATED INTEREST

In SELF-ESTEEM/A DECLARATION, world-renowned family therapist Virginia Satir presents an essential credo for the individual in modern society. 64 pages, soft cover,$2.95

In MAKING CONTACT, Virginia Satir draws on years of experience and observation, and a rich understanding of human potential and interaction, to show how you can better understand and use the basic tools for making contact with others. She clearly explains reliable techniques that will make it possible for you to work for change in your perceptions, your actions, and your life. 96 pages, soft cover, $3.95

SELECTIVE AWARENESS by Dr. Peter H.C. Mutke demonstrates the power of selective awareness in reprogramming negative thought/ emotion patterns to promote physical health, healing, and the undoing of destructive habits such as overeating, smoking, insomnia, and pain. 240 pages, soft cover, $4.95

In SELF-CARE, Yetta Bernhard tells her reader to say "I count," and describes exactly how to put the premises of self-care into practical, everyday living. 252 pages, soft cover, $6.95

POSITIVE SELFISHNESS by Frieda Porat, Ph.D. addresses the central problem in the search for self-fulfillment: self-esteem. It encourages readers to recognize their own special qualities and abilities, affirm them, and build upon them. The author provides specific exercises that will allow readers to see their own problems in perspective and enable them to understand the dynamics of a healthy love of self. 172 pages, soft cover, $4.95

IT'S UP TO YOU is Eileen D. Gambrill and Cheryl A. Richey's basic handbook for developing assertive social skills. Particular attention is devoted to basics: where to go to meet people, handling conversations, arranging meetings, evaluating contacts and making positive changes. 156 pages, soft cover, $4.95

In THE INWARD JOURNEY, art therapist Margaret Frings Keyes integrates Gestalt techniques with Transactional Analysis and Jungian thought in a rich and illuminating guide for the lay reader to the use of art as therapy. 128 pages, soft cover, $4.95

In HOW TO BE SOMEBODY, noted psychologist Yetta Bernhard presents a specific guide for personal growth that will "lead to acceptance of one's self as a human being." 128 pages, soft cover, $3.95

Available at your local book or department store or directly from the publisher. To order by mail, send check or money order to:

Celestial Arts
231 Adrian Road
Suite MPB
Millbrae, Ca 94030

Please include 50 cents for postage and handling. California residents add 6% tax.